ST ERKENWALD

EXETER MEDIEVAL TEXTS AND STUDIES

Series Editors:
Richard Dance, University of Cambridge
and Eddie Jones, University of Exeter

Editorial Committee:
Margaret Connolly, University of St Andrews
Susan Irvine, University College London
Bella Millett, University of Southampton
Sarah Peverley, University of Liverpool
Sue Powell, University of Leeds
Ad Putter, University of Bristol
William Robins, University of Toronto

Editors Emeritus:
M.J. Swanton (founder)
Marion Glasscoe
Vincent Gillespie

St Erkenwald

A Critical Edition

THORLAC TURVILLE-PETRE

LIVERPOOL UNIVERSITY PRESS

First published in 2024 by
Liverpool University Press
4 Cambridge Street
Liverpool
L69 7ZU

This paperback edition published 2026

Copyright © 2026 Thorlac Turville-Petre

Thorlac Turville-Petre has asserted the right to be identified as the author of this book in accordance with the Copyright, Designs and Patents Act 1988.

All rights reserved. No part of this book may be reproduced, stored in a retrieval system, or transmitted, in any form or by any means, electronic, mechanical, photocopying, recording, or otherwise, without the prior written permission of the publisher.

British Library Cataloguing-in-Publication data
A British Library CIP record is available

ISBN 978-1-80207-444-4 (hardback)
ISBN 978-1-80596-749-1 (paperback)

Typeset by Carnegie Book Production, Lancaster

Contents

Acknowledgements   vi

Abbreviations   vii

Introduction   1
  1. The Poem and Its Editions   1
  2. The Manuscript   3
  3. Author and Audience   12
  4. Sources   19
  5. Theology: Heaven and Hell   27
  6. Language and Vocabulary   35
  7. Metre   38
  8. Structure and Style   44
  9. Treatment of the Text   52

Bibliography   53

Translation, Text and Variants   61

Annotations   83

Appendix: The Glosses   107

Glossary   111

Index of Names   139

Acknowledgements

I am very grateful to the series editors, Richard Dance and Eddie Jones, for their many valuable comments and suggestions. The teams at Liverpool University Press and Carnegie Book Production have been immensely helpful and patient. As always, Clare Litt guided the edition expertly through to publication.

Parts of the Introduction have appeared in *The Chaucer Review* and *Nottingham Medieval Studies*.

Abbreviations

AN	Anglo-Norman
ChR	*Chaucer Review*
CT	Chaucer's *Canterbury Tales*
DIMEV	*Digital Index of Middle English Verse*, dimev.net
DT	*The Destruction of Troy*
EETS	Early English Text Society
OS	Original Series
SS	Supplementary Series
Gawain	*Sir Gawain and the Green Knight*
Gersum	gersum.org
JEGP	*Journal of English and Germanic Philology*
LALME	*A Linguistic Atlas of Late Mediaeval English*, ed. Angus McIntosh et al., 4 vols (Aberdeen, 1986)
MÆ	*Medium Ævum*
MED	*Middle English Dictionary*
MP	*Modern Philology*
N&Q	*Notes and Queries*
ODNB	*Oxford Dictionary of National Biography*, oxforddnb.com
OE	Old English
OED	*Oxford English Dictionary*, oed.com
OF	Old French
ON	Old Norse
PL	*Patrologia Latina*, ed. J.-P. Migne
SEL	*South English Legendary*
Siege	*The Siege of Jerusalem*

TNA   The National Archives
VCH   Victoria County History
Wars   The Wars of Alexander
Wynnere Wynnere and Wastoure

Introduction

1. The Poem and Its Editions

As Christianity is re-established in seventh-century Britain and the old pagan temples are rebuilt and rededicated to Christian saints, workmen digging deep into the foundations of St Paul's cathedral unearth a remarkable tomb, decorated with strange symbols and containing a body, perfectly preserved and dressed in the robes of a judge, wearing a crown and holding a sceptre. With consternation mixed with curiosity, the city officials summon Erkenwald, bishop of London. Instead of examining the tomb, Erkenwald spends the night alone in prayer. The next morning, after celebrating high mass, he is led to the tomb, where the dean of St Paul's explains that, despite their careful researches through the cathedral records, they can find no reference to identify this body. Addressing the assembly of clerics and nobles, the bishop admonishes them saying that what is an impossibility for human minds is easily resolved by God.

Then Erkenwald turns to question the corpse: 'Who are you?' The body replies that in the distant past, centuries before the birth of Christ, he administered justice in the pagan city, and acted so admirably that the citizens buried him with the crown and sceptre as the king of judges. 'Then your excellent conduct must have reaped you a rich reward. What of your soul in heaven?' 'Alas, my soul is sorrowing in darkness. Good deeds earned me nothing in the absence of faith.' At this, Erkenwald is deeply troubled, and wishes that the judge might last until he is able to fetch water and say: 'I baptise you in the name of the Father, the Son and the Holy Spirit'. Weeping as he utters the words of baptism, he lets fall a tear on the judge's face. Praising God, the judge says that at this baptism his soul sprang up to heaven to join the company of the blessed seated at the heavenly banquet. Having spoken these words, the body crumbles at once to dust. With great rejoicing, Erkenwald leads the procession away, as the bells of the city miraculously ring in unison.

St Erkenwald is 'a dramatic and powerful retelling of a miracle at St Paul's, densely evocative in its language, full of awe, mystery and sadness'.[1] The text was first printed in 1881 by Carl Horstmann, and the first separate edition with full introduction and apparatus by Sir Israel Gollancz was published in 1922 in his series *Select Early English Poems*. Gollancz was too eager to emend in cases of difficulty, and many of his emendations are unnecessary. The three editions that followed all began as doctoral dissertations, with the virtues of enthusiasm and the vices of inexperience. The meticulous edition by Henry Savage (1926) set out the poem in four-line stanzas, following Gollancz. The edition by Ruth Morse (1975) was followed two years later by Clifford Peterson's (1977), who supplied a comprehensive introduction and apparatus. Gollancz, Savage and Peterson expanded the flourishes on final consonants as -e. Two further editions in anthologies by Turville-Petre (1989) and by Burrow and Turville-Petre (1992, 2021) inevitably offer much briefer annotations.

The resources for the editor have expanded significantly in recent years and so the poem is due for a new edition. The completion of the *Middle English Dictionary* is a magnificent achievement: when Peterson edited the poem in 1977 it was about to enter the letter N. Every editor needs to refer to *MED*'s display of the meanings and distribution of words. Like *MED*, *OED* is now online and undergoing major revision. The Gersum Project, launched in 2016, traces Scandinavian vocabulary in alliterative poems including *St Erkenwald* in more detail than previously attempted, which is particularly valuable for words of uncertain origin and meaning; see, for example, the note on *skelton* (278). Other internet resources include digitisation of manuscripts, one of which is BL MS Harley 2250 with the unique text of *St Erkenwald*. The *Linguistic Atlas of Later Mediaeval English* (*LALME*) appeared in print in 1986, and it too is now online. It is invaluable for the study of Middle English dialects and enables the placement of the English texts of Harley 2250 with new precision, so that they take their place in relation to other Cheshire writings. In a series of seminal studies beginning in 1982, Gordon Whatley explored other texts concerning Erkenwald, including liturgies, and traced in great detail the relation of the poem to its analogues, in particular the legend of the emperor Trajan. Previous editors of *St Erkenwald* had an imperfect understanding of alliterative metre, but a series of studies from the late 1980s by Hoyt N. Duggan and Thomas Cable, and by Ad Putter et al. in 2007, have been of

---

[1] Pearsall 1977, p. 176.

particular value to the editor, so that the text of *St Erkenwald* may more confidently be established, particularly in relation to the value of final *-e*.[2] Finally, there were not many interpretative studies of the poem until the beginning of this century, since when they have proliferated.[3]

From the outset editors have been much exercised over whether the *Gawain* poet wrote *St Erkenwald*. (This assumes, as is the general consensus, that *Pearl*, *Cleanness*, *Patience* and *Gawain* are all by one author.) Gollancz bizarrely thought that *St Erkenwald* 'is such that the author of *Cleanness* and *Patience* might well have written when his powers were faltering' (p. lx), and identified the writer as Ralph Strode. Savage devoted twenty-five pages to the question, pointing to similar passages and common stylistic traits. Peterson, noting the name Thomas Masse in the manuscript, attempted to prove that a certain John Massey of Cotton wrote all five poems. None of the editors came up with conclusive arguments. Objecting that single authorship made *St Erkenwald* 'a stepchild which could with reason be neglected', Morse (p. 47) summarily dismissed the arguments in its favour. All that can now be said with certainty is that, whatever else the poet may have written, *St Erkenwald* can confidently stand on its own and be read and enjoyed for its own sake.

2. The Manuscript

BL Ms Harley 2250 consists of two unrelated manuscripts bound together. References to 'the manuscript' are to the first of these, folios 1–87.[4] This consists of a miscellany of religious texts in English and

---

[2] For a conspectus of the current state of play in alliterative metrical studies, advancing new theories, confirming some previous views and contesting others, see the essays in *The Chaucer Review* 58.2 (2023), 147–282.

[3] See in particular Borroff 2006b, Bugbee 2008, Grady 2005, Kerby-Fulton 2021, Salih 2019, Scattergood 2017, Sisk 2007.

[4] Images of the complete manuscript are available online at https://www.bl.uk/manuscripts/FullDisplay.aspx?ref=Harley_MS_2250. The English text in the second part of the manuscript, ff. 88–108, is a treatise on the Ten Commandments and the Seven Sins, drawing on the *Memoriale Credencium* and the *Charter of the Abbey of the Holy Ghost*, which appear in simplified and abbreviated form. It begins on ff. 88r–90v.ii with an unidentified text, inc. 'For als mykell as ilk man while he lifs here in þis worlde ...' describing life as a pilgrimage and stating that whether our destination is heaven or hell will depend on our obeying the commandments, which follow. On f. 90v.ii, within the fourth commandment, the source switches to *MC*, p. 44. The section on the sins and their remedies begins with Pride on

Latin, written in one main hand, with brief additions in other hands. Its principal contents are *A Stanzaic Life of Christ* in English, the *Speculum Christiani* in English and Latin, extracts from the *Dieta Salutis*, *St Erkenwald*, lives from the *South English Legendary* and sermons and extracts from Mirk's *Festial*. The contents are all on religious topics, the majority widely available in multiple copies. The manuscript represents a practical miscellany in English and Latin made for, perhaps by, a parish priest of the later fifteenth century. A more detailed analysis of contents is given below.[5]

History

LALME distinguishes three Cheshire dialects of the main scribe's English texts.[6] Marginalia indicate that the manuscript was not only copied in Cheshire but that it was owned and in use locally for many years. Two names in particular are informative: the first is 'Ser Thomas boker hos [has] Thys boke' (f. 8r), repeated on f. 71r as 'Syr Thomas bowker', to which has been added 'mine emys' [my uncle]; the second is in a trial introduction to a bond, 'Nouerint vniuersi per presentes nos Eesebyt bothe of dunnam in the comytye of chester in the comythe' (f. 75v). The Booths of Dunham Massey were a prominent Cheshire family, and Elizabeth is probably to be identified as the wife of George Booth, for she would have been in a position to conduct transactions after her husband's death in 1531 until 1541, while the heir was a minor.[7] Thomas Bowker is named in three wills. In 1520/1 Margaret Hawarden of Chester

---

f. 92r.i (*MC*, p. 52, l. 8) and runs through to f. 93v, ending mid-sentence in Meekness (*MC*, p. 66 l. 6). There follow three leaves, originally blank but ruled, on the last of which, f. 94r, has been written the Latin Constitution of Robert Winchelsea. F. 95r begins mid-sentence in the account of Charity (*MC*, p. 82, l. 1) and ends in the middle of Penance on f. 105v.ii (*MC*, p. 157 l. 19), moving directly on to the rubric 'Memorandum quod primo die incarnacionis homini' (*Charter*, p. 340), continuing with Satan's apostasy and Christ's redemption of mankind: '3e shall vnderstand þat þer was a false tyrant þat hight Sathanas …'. The extract ends on f. 108r.ii with 'ledde þem into þe blise of heven þat neuer shall haue ende Amen' (*Charter*, p. 362). The watermark is similar to Briquet 15068, dated 1462. *LALME* identifies the hand as LP 217 from Yorkshire West Riding.

[5] For further characterisation of the contents of Harley 2250 see Turville-Petre 2023b.

[6] *LALME* 1, p. 111, identifies three varieties, presumably reflecting the dialects of the scribe's exemplars: ff. 1r–47v *Stanzaic Life* LP 17 NE Cheshire; ff. 72v–75v *St Erkenwald* LP 419 SE Cheshire; 84r–87v *Festial* probably NE Cheshire.

[7] The records are analysed by Luttrell 1958, 38–42.

bequeathed twenty pence to him, and in 1527/8 Elizabeth Hurleston requested that 'my prest Sir Thomas Bowker shall syng ffor us yff he be able'.[8] Both women had family connections with the Booths.[9] In 1526 Thomas Bowker was a witness to the will of John Booth of the branch of the family at Barton-on-Irwell, Lancs.[10] John Booth, whose wife Dorothy was Elizabeth's sister, requested burial in the church at Eccles by Barton-on-Irwell, where the Booths had established the chantry of St Katherine in 1450 and the chantry of Jesus and St Mary the Virgin in 1460; in his will of 1464 Archbishop William Booth had made a bequest for a house for chantry priests.[11] In 1535 Thomas Boweker was named as first cantarist at the Jesus and Mary chantry. He was dead by 1538.[12] Other names in the manuscript are 'Willyam Barton' (f. 75v) and 'Thomas Masse, Thomas Masse esquier' (f. 13r), repeated on f. 64v. A Thomas Massye, gentleman, is another witness to John Booth's will. In later years a reader went painstakingly through the English texts, glossing words that had become obsolete, nearly always accurately.

Thus the first identifiable owner of the manuscript was Thomas Bowker, who was associated with the Booths, particularly the Barton branch of the family, in the earlier sixteenth century. Though it is not certain when it entered the Harley collection, Humphrey Wanley (d. 1726) described it as it now stands, as two separate manuscripts bound together.[13]

Physical Description

The volume consists of 111 paper leaves. At beginning and end are two modern endpapers and a flyleaf. Folios 44a (a fragment) and 93a and 93b (ruled but blank) are not numbered, so the last leaf is numbered 108. In part I of the volume there are two foliations; the earlier numbered the fragment 44a as f. 1, but when the volume was rebound

---

[8] *Lancashire and Cheshire Wills* 2, pp. 6–12; *Lancashire and Cheshire Wills* 1, pp. 35–8.

[9] Luttrell 1958, 41.

[10] *Lancashire and Cheshire Wills* 1, pp. 14–16. Thomas Booth of Barton (d. c. 1454) was brother of Robert of Dunham Massey (d. 1450); also brother of William, archbishop of York, and half-brother of Laurence, bishop of Durham.

[11] *History of the Chantries*, pp. 131–9; *ODNB*, 'Booth [Bothe], William (d. 1464), archbishop of York'.

[12] *Valor Ecclesiasticus* V, p. 227, cited by Luttrell 1958, 40; *VCH Lancaster* IV, p. 361.

[13] *A Catalogue of the Harleian Collection of Manuscripts*, ed. Wanley 1759, II, pp. 577–8.

this fragment was misplaced between ff. 44 and 45, and the earlier f. 2 renumbered as f. 1, with that numeration carried on through the volume.[14] On f. 87v is written 'In this book are 88 folia'. The second manuscript in the volume therefore runs from f. 88 to f. 108. The leaves measure approx. 290 × 205 mm. When the volume was rebound in the nineteenth century the quires were split and the leaves individually mounted. There are no quire signatures, so that it is not possible to determine the collation. The watermarks in part I resemble Briquet 9183, a letter Y with a trefoil tail, dated 1473. This date accords well with the date 1477 in a colophon on f. 64v at the end of *Speculum Christiani* in the hand of the main scribe.

The main texts of part I are in one hand, with brief fillers by two or three other fifteenth-century hands. There is no decoration, with simple rubrication of enlarged initials, capitals sometimes dabbed in red, and some words underlined in red. The leaf is ruled to the left of the text block and under the top line only, so the script, an untidy secretary, is unevenly aligned. It is clearly a manuscript intended for practical use rather than display.

St Erkenwald begins at the top of f. 72v, with the rubricated title *De Erkenwaldo*, which is the heading throughout the text, and a two-line rubricated first letter. There is no other decoration of any sort except a two-line capital on f. 74r, at the beginning of l. 177.

Contents of the Manuscript

1r–47v: *A Stanzaic Life of Christ* (untitled). Defective at beginning and end and omitting ll. 693–1173. Two columns. *DIMEV* 2908 lists three copies. Ed. Foster, EETS 166 (1926). The text begins with a fragment previously numbered 1 but now bound in as f. 44a, containing on 44av parts of lines 624–92, jumping to 1174–9, and on 44ar parts of lines 1202–55 and 1277–304 (with omissions). The new f. 1 (previously numbered 2) begins with l. 1331, 'Jesus wos gefen hym by reson', and the text breaks off with the Latin rubric following l. 10,840, 'Orante Jesu descendit spiritus sanctus & cetera'. From l. 9625 this becomes Foster's copytext, with the later part of the poem lost in the other two copies. The end of the poem is missing in all three mss.

48r–49v: 'De Sancto Martino': 'Saynt Martyne wos borene in þe londe of Sabarie … Now god gife vs part of þat ioy þat his soule is jnne

---

[14] Wanley noticed the misplaced leaf which 'the negligent Book-binder hath inserted between the Leaves 44 & 45'.

jdo'. *DIMEV* 4695 lists seventeen copies. *SEL*, ed. d'Evelyn and Mill, pp. 483–92. Abbreviated version, as in Bodley Ashmole MS 43 and BL MS Egerton 2810. See Görlach 1974, p. 202. Fol. 49 is a part leaf.

49v: Five lines in another hand, Latin, based on *Elucidarium*, 2.20 (*PL* 172.1150), on ways to distinguish good from evil, inc. 'Boni et mali aliquibus signis poterunt nosci'. Followed by Latin scribbles. Below that, in a third hand, English from Mirk's *Festial* (see below) 55.21-9, quoting Chrysostom on the merit of tears of contrition: 'Johannes Crisostomus O þou teere þat art mekely lettyn … þus þow paynest þe fende worse þen he myght haue payned the'. The first lines are recopied by a fourth hand.

50r-64v: 'Speculum Christiani' (title in later hand): 'Evangelium qui ex deo est uerba dei audit … qui ad amorem eius plurimos trahit. Libro Finito assint laudes deo amen'. Ed. Holmstedt, EETS 182 (1933). There are over fifty manuscript copies and at least seven early prints. Latin and English. *DIMEV* indexes English verses as 5845, 6643, 3492. Single cols. From 'septima tabula' (Holmstedt, p. 133) to the end, all the English is dropped. Colophon: 'Explicit Speculum Christiani anno domini m° cccc^{mo} lxxvii°'. Beside that in another hand: 'Quidem anima obiecta incorporea nullo colore colorata omnibus organis circumspecta creatori assimulata'.

64v-68r: 'Hic incipiunt themata dominicalia', commonly attached to William of Lavicia's *Dieta salutis*. Inc. 'Abiciamus opera tenebrarum et induamur arma lucis. Romanos 13. In adventu magni regis et principis expiantur sordes …'. *S. Bonaventurae opera omnia*, ed. Peltier, 8.347–58.

68r-72r: 'Vltima tabula diete salutis continens diuisiones membrorum', two columns. *Tabula* that follows *Dieta salutis*. Latin.

72rb: Lists of articles of faith, sacraments, commandments, deadly sins, works of corporal mercy, works of spiritual mercy. Latin. Seventeen lines at foot in another hand: 'Deus est ubique potencialiter, in altari sacramentaliter, in celo localiter … ad deus non attendit'. Direct source not identified.

72v-75v: 'De Erkenwaldo': 'At london in Englond noȝt full long sythen … And all þe belles in þe burgh beryd at ones'. *DIMEV* 706.

75v-76v: 'De sancto Johanne baptista': 'Saynt John þe beste barne þe holy baptyste … & after his dethe wide wenten cristendome to lere'. *DIMEV* 4647 lists eighteen copies. A variant version of *SEL* pp. 241–6, ed. Newhauser and Bolton 2012. See Görlach 1974, pp. 176 and 280 n.199.

77r–77v: 'de sancto Albano': 'Saynt Albane þe holy mon wos her of englonde ... þat we mowen com at oure endyng to þe ioy þat euer shal last amen'. *DIMEV* 4534 lists seventeen copies. *SEL* pp. 238–41; see Görlach 1974, pp. 174–5.

77v: 'de sancto Juliano confessor': 'Saynt Julian þe confessour borne was in rome ... quen men ben gon in strong stydde & of herbare ben agast'. *DIMEV* 4651 lists nineteen copies. *SEL* pp. 31–2; see Görlach 1974, p. 140.

77v–78v: 'De sancto Juliano hospite': 'Saynt Julian þe noble herbargeour of noble kynne he come ... þat god vs graunte þrogh oure seruice þat gate þat Julian ȝede'. *DIMEV* 4652 lists twenty-two copies. *SEL* pp. 32–7; see Görlach 1974, pp. 140–1.

79r–80v: 'De cruce': 'The holy rode þat swete tre gode is to haue in mynde ... For to wende to Jerusalem þe holy rode to seche'. *DIMEV* 5339 lists twenty-two copies. *SEL* pp. 167–74; see Görlach 1974, pp. 164–6.

80v–81r: 'Inuencio sancte crucis': 'Qwen Elene come to Jerusalem seche a rede ho nome ... Þat we mowen to þe ioy come of heuen þat is so gode Amen'. *DIMEV* 133 lists eighteen copies. *SEL* pp. 174–8 (but divided from 'De cruce' at l. 227). See Görlach 1974, pp. 164–6.

81r–v: 'Saynt quyriak': 'Saynt quyriak þe bisshop prechid goddes lawe ... Saynt elene & Saynt quyriak to heuen riche os brynge'. *DIMEV* 4754. *SEL* pp. 179–80. Görlach 1974, p. 166, lists eighteen copies.

81v–83r: 'Saynt Elene': 'Seynt elene was in bretayn borne & come of hegh kynrade ... Oure lorde for saynt elene loue sende vs heuen blis Amen'. *DIMEV* 4613 lists one other copy. Ed. Harbus 2002, *Helena of Britain*, appendix 2. See Görlach 1974, p. 166.

83r–v: 'Exaltacio sancte crucis', beginning in double columns. 'The holy rode þat was founden as ȝe weten in may ... Brynge vs to the hegh ioy þat yow boght vs to Amen'. *DIMEV* 5338 lists nineteen copies. *SEL* pp. 390–7. See Görlach 1974, pp. 91, 190, 251 n.107.

83v: 'Raby moyses sayes þat hit is as ferre from erth ...', three lines in another hand on the distance from earth to heaven. From Mirk's *Festial* 37.30–3. Below that three lines in a third hand, a remedy 'For þe axys' (*MED acces(se*, 'ague').

84r–v: Mirk's sermon for Corpus Christi: 'Gode men and wommen ȝe shall knawe well ... The quyche god graunte vs to Amen'. Two columns. *Festial* 41.

84vb: 'Now the lawe is lad by clere consciens … Now regneth truteh [sic] in euery mannys syght'. Eight-line punctuation poem on the evils of the time, in a later hand. *DIMEV* 3804 lists six copies. Ed. Kreuzer 1938; and cf. Robbins, *Secular Lyrics*, pp. 101, 263. Seven lines at the foot are too faded to be legible.

85r-v: Sermon for Maundy Thursday/Easter Eve, two columns, heading 'Deus expediat me', as in e.g. Leeds UL, Brotherton MS 205, f. 17v. Inc. 'Hit is ofte sene þat lewed men quich ben of many wordes … in the passion of crist the quych is oure helthe & so forthe'. Adds Latin rubrics; *Festial* 28. This copy printed Young 1936.

85v-86va: 'De festo apostolorum Philippi et Jacobi, sermo breuis', two columns, inc. 'Gode men & wemen such a day 3e schal haue … come to the blis þat þes apostils ben in Amen', *Festial* 32.

86va-b: *Narracio* from Sermon for St Andrew: 'Narracio de miraculo Sancti Andree quomodo diabolus apparuit Sancto Cutberto in specie mulieris', in two columns, 'Hit fell þat þer was a bisshop þat loued wele Saynt Andrew … and preche vnto þe peple in helpe of hom Amen'. *Festial* 2.118-76. Only here is the bishop to whom the devil appeared named as St Cuthbert.

86vb: *Narracio* from sermon for Lent, in two columns: 'Narracio I rede þer wer ij chapmen dwellyng beside the cyte of Northwiche … whiche joy god graunte 3ow and me amen', *Festial* 34, 191-232.

86vb-87rb: *Narracio* from sermon for Invention of the Cross, in two columns: 'Narracio As I rede I fynd þat in a cite þat wos callid beritus … þe blis þat he boght vs to hongyng þeron amen', *Festial* 33, 87-136, with five additional lines. Fol. 86 is damaged with loss of text.

87rb: *Narracio* from sermon for Nativity of the Virgin, in two columns: 'Narracio I rede in þe myraculs of our lady how þer was a jewe þat was born in fraunce … and bryng 3ow to þe ioy [*lost*] schall laste Amen', *Festial* 57, 120-53, with three additional lines. Fol. 87 is damaged with loss of text. Seven Latin lines at foot in another hand, inc. 'Nota quod propter nouem raciones prodest homini audire missam', found also in e.g. CUL MS Ee.4.35, f. 24r.

87va: Two notes in English in another hand, the first on terms for units of time, 'lustrum', 'indicion', 'seculum', 'evum', 'þe grete cicle of Plato', inc. 'Fyfe 3ere makes lustrum, þat is the space of v 3ere'. Followed by 'De temporibus diei naturalis', fragmentary, found also in e.g. Harley MS 218, ff. 73v-74r.

87vb: Latin sermon notes, not main hand, faded, citing Bede's commentary on Genesis 3.8 (*PL* 91, 0056A). Below that, in yet another hand, very faded and largely illegible, brief English account of the ages of the world, inc. 'In þe begynnyng god made heuen and erthe'.

Character and Circulation of the Texts

The first text in the manuscript as it now stands, the *Stanzaic Life of Christ*, was composed by a Cheshire cleric, probably a Benedictine from St Werburgh's Abbey, and there is no evidence that it circulated widely. It survives incomplete in two other manuscripts and it was a source of some plays in the *Chester Mystery Cycle*. The poem draws on material from two greatly prized Latin works: the *Polychronicon*, written at St Werburgh's in the 1340s by Ranulf Higden, and the *Legenda Aurea*, by Jacobus de Voragine, composed in the 1260s. In this way the poem sets the life of Christ in the context of 'universal history', as in the *Polychronicon*, and also in episodes corresponding to the great feasts of the Church, as in *Legenda Aurea*. It is composed in simple cross-rhyme quatrains, using an everyday vocabulary, so that the poem is easy to follow and easy to remember. For the clerkly reader Latin headings are provided at the top of the page with Latin summaries of the action to follow, just perfect for the priest looking for material suitable 'For lewed men þat here ben by' (f. 28v).

On fols. 50r–64v is the *Speculum Christiani*, a handbook of pastoral care that proved immensely popular, surviving in over fifty manuscripts.[15] In the prologue the author reminds the reader of John Pecham's Lambeth Constitutions of 1281, *Ignorantia Sacerdotum*, requiring parishioners to be instructed four times a year in the elements of the faith. The work is then loosely divided into eight *tabulae*, the first four of which cover the Creed, the commandments, the sins, the works of mercy and the virtues. Much of the *Speculum* is written in Latin, interspersed with simple English quatrains. The fifth *tabula* is in English with Latin citations, opening with a sermon: 'My dere frendes I ȝow pray four thynges beres in ȝour hertes away' (f. 55r). The sixth is a retelling of the Sayings of the Four Philosophers, and the seventh again focuses on sinfulness. The *Speculum* is prepared for the priest rather than directly for his parishioners, so that the eighth *tabula* begins with the duties of priesthood and includes an explanation of the symbolism of vestments.[16] In this copy numerous passages have been omitted, and

---

[15] See Gillespie 2008.
[16] See Gillespie 1980.

it is difficult for users to negotiate their way around, since the *ordinatio* of the page is basic, there are no running heads and the *tabulae* are not indicated or separated.

Following material associated with *Dieta Salutis* are selections from the *South English Legendary*. The earliest copies dating from the end of the thirteenth century can be located in Worcestershire and Gloucestershire.[17] The text spread widely, and was revised, adapted and expanded throughout the following 250 years. The loose septenary couplets were an easy medium for the least competent versifier to adopt and adapt. Its sources include the *Legenda Aurea*. The *Legendary* was popular, surviving in some twenty-six 'major manuscripts' plus miscellanies containing individual legends, and fragments.[18] Of the ten legends in Harley 2250, all are extant in multiple copies, apart from Elene (Helena). The two manuscripts that are textually closest to Harley 2250 are BL MS Egerton 2810 and Lambeth Palace Library MS 223, both with Cheshire connections.

John Mirk's sermon collection, the *Festial*, is the last work copied by the main scribe. Mirk was a canon at the Augustinian abbey at Lilleshall in Shropshire. He wrote his *Festial* in the 1380s, drawing especially on the *Legenda Aurea*. With its set of sixty-four sermons and lively *narrationes* it was deservedly popular, surviving in twenty-one complete manuscripts and prints by Caxton and Wynkyn de Worde, as well as revised versions and sixteen miscellanies containing selections.[19] Though the *Festial* was copied quite widely, its circulation was non-metropolitan, like the other English texts in Harley 2250, until the advent of printing. One group of manuscripts circulated in the west and south-west Midlands, another group in the east Midland counties of Leicestershire and Nottinghamshire. Harley 2250 seems to be the most northern copy extant.

In many ways *St Erkenwald* is distinct from the other contents of the manuscript. Unlike Mirk's *narrationes*, it is too long and complex to serve as a sermon *exemplum*. Like the *Stanzaic Life*, it is a local composition, but its verse form is very different, for it is written in unrhymed alliterative verse in an area where the alliterative tradition was strongest. Alliterative verse, with its special vocabulary and stylistic techniques, was hardly composed for the instruction of the unsophisticated audience who needed visual images as 'lewed mennus bokys', in Mirk's words.

---

[17] Görlach 1974 is an essential study.
[18] Görlach 1974, pp. viii–x.
[19] See Mirk, ed. Powell 2009, pp. xlviii–xlix.

The compiler of Harley 2250 assembled texts that were of use to a parish priest, both to inform himself and to instruct his congregation. The *South English Legendary*, the *Speculum Christiani* and the *Festial* originated in the south-west and central Midlands, and circulated widely to a non-metropolitan audience and were likely to have been readily available in Cheshire as elsewhere in the Midlands. However, the *Stanzaic Life of Christ* and *St Erkenwald*, both Cheshire compositions, had a much more local circulation, if the surviving manuscripts are any guide. This restricted circulation may indicate a certain exclusiveness in vernacular culture in Cheshire. Though Cheshire scribes imported works from other parts of the Midlands, Cheshire compositions apparently had limited currency in the wider world.

3. Author and Audience

In or shortly after 1396 John Tickhill, collector of the rents of the dean and chapter of St Paul's, used the blank space on his rent roll to write forty-one lines of passable alliterative verse, probably of his own composition, describing the narrator's forlorn encounter in Bishopswood with a mournful, mateless bird.[20] Tickhill may have come from the town of that name in Yorkshire, or his family may have resided in London for several generations. The purported evidence of northern dialect in the poem is insubstantial and probably represents the mixed dialect of London, with its steady influx of immigrants,[21] while the influence of Langland is evident both in its vocabulary and its formulas. This, coupled with the *chanson d'aventure* opening, characterises the poem as an experimental pastiche rather than a serious work of original merit.

It has been suggested that the author of *St Erkenwald*, who centres his poem on London and St Paul's, may, like Tickhill, have had a position there as a member of the minor clergy, perhaps a chantry clerk.[22] While that is a possibility, the differences between the two poems make any comparison misleading. Most importantly, the author of *Erkenwald* was clearly not writing for his own amusement, but for an audience and presumably for a patron.

---

[20] *A Bird in Bishopswood*, edited and discussed by Kennedy 1987.
[21] See Burnley 1983, pp. 108–32; Horobin 2017.
[22] Kerby-Fulton 2021, pp. 261–97, who makes the connection with Tickhill's lines. She also argues that the author must have had intimate knowledge of St Paul's, which seems to me unproven.

Indeed, *Erkenwald* is not a London poem, as it is often described, any more than *Wynnere and Wastoure* is. Both poems focus on London – 'Chese þe forthe into þe Chepe, a chamber þou rere' ['Go out into Cheapside and fix up a room'] (*Wynnere* 474) – but both are written from a distance. The narrator of *Wynnere* is a 'westren wy' who dare not 'send his sone southewarde' (7–8), i.e. to the Great Wen. In the first line of his poem the author of *Erkenwald* announces that the action takes place 'At London in Englond'.[23] Here, at the outset, the narrator distances himself from both London and England and proclaims a distinctive regional identity, for Cestrians saw Cheshire as separate from England.[24] As a County Palatine, Cheshire was exempt from national taxation and sent no representatives to parliament until 1543. When, in 1450, Cheshire was commanded to pay a tax granted by parliament, the 'Abbotes, Priours, and all the Clergy, Barons, Knyghtes, Squiers, and all the comialtee of your comite palatyne of Chestre' petitioned Henry VI, setting out the ways in which the 'comite is and hath ben a comite palatyne als well afore the conquest of Englond as sithen, distincte and seperate from youre coron of Englond',[25] and the king was obliged to reaffirm the 'liberties, freedoms and franchises' of the county.[26] Though some of the claims were specious or exaggerated, it remains the case that Cheshire's 'status as a palatinate did give it a separateness from the rest of the country'.[27] Henry Bradshaw (d. 1513), a monk of St Werburgh's Abbey, praised the beauty and sweet wholesomeness of Chester and the virtue and prosperity of its citizens, and described how William the Conqueror had granted the earl of Chester and his successors the right 'to calle a parlement to his wyll and syght, / To ordre his subiectes after true iustice / As a prepotent prince' (*Life of St Werburge*, 2.1273–5).

A Londoner, who could have understood Tickhill's lines with ease, would have found *St Erkenwald* decidedly difficult, especially its vocabulary, composed as it is in the high alliterative style of northern poets. This style called upon a specialised vocabulary of 'high alliterative rank', the range of nouns for 'man, knight', verbs for 'go, move', idealising adjectives and so on, which was shared with other alliterative

---

[23] See Burrow 1993.
[24] See Clayton 1990.
[25] Printed and discussed by Harrod 1900; quotation on p. 75.
[26] Harrod 1900, 78; Clayton 1990, p. 48.
[27] Clayton 1990, p. 63.

works from the north, particularly *Gawain* and its companions and the *Wars of Alexander*.[28]

It follows that the proposal that the poem was commissioned in 1386 by the bishop of London, Robert Braybrooke, in his drive to promote the veneration of Erkenwald is unpersuasive.[29] For the same reason, the suggestion that it was composed for the Erkenwald guild in London is implausible.[30] Though the cult centred on London, it was not confined to the city, as evidenced by images of the saint in manuscripts and painted glass from as far afield as Norwich, Lincolnshire and Somerset, and the copy of the *Vita sancti Erkenwaldi* owned by Holme Cultram Abbey in Cumbria.[31] It seems most probable that *St Erkenwald* was commissioned with a Cheshire audience in view by someone with strong Cheshire affiliations, who may of course also have been active in the affairs of St Paul's. In this context we have seen that marginalia in the manuscript direct attention to the Booths. John Booth of Barton (d. 1422) served as a member of parliament and two of his sons, William and his younger half-brother Laurence, who became archbishop of York and bishop of Durham respectively, were active at St Paul's, as prebendary from 1421 in William's case, and in Laurence's case as residentiary canon from 1450 and dean in 1456–7.[32] To suggest that they commissioned or encouraged the composition of *St Erkenwald* would be to date the poem later than generally accepted, but the Booth brothers perhaps represent the kind of involvement between Cheshire and the metropolis to have inspired *St Erkenwald*. Whatever the case, the Booths would surely have had an interest in preserving a sophisticated poem about Erkenwald, bishop of London.

It is not possible to date the poem at all closely except on stylistic grounds, but the features of style that it shares with the *Gawain* poems, usually dated 1380–1400, are so striking that it seems unlikely that it was written a generation or more later. Those shared features are suggestive enough to raise the question of single authorship, which receives support from *LALME*'s placing of the dialects of Cotton Nero A.x (LP 26) and the copy of *Erkenwald* (LP 419) a few miles apart in east Cheshire. Of course, these are scribal dialects, but there is no

---

[28] See below, pp. 37–8.
[29] An argument revived by Barron 2003.
[30] Suggested by Duffy 2018.
[31] Whatley 1989, pp. 1–2, 69. The window on the cover of this book is in Norwich.
[32] *ODNB*, 'Booth [Bothe], Laurence'; 'Booth [Bothe], William (d. 1464)'.

reason to suspect that they grossly misrepresent the authorial texts. An argument frequently made to support the single authorship of the Cotton Nero poems is, as A. C. Spearing puts it, that 'it is easier to believe that towards the end of the fourteenth century, within a certain rather small dialect area, there lived one great poet than to believe that there lived two, or three, or four'.[33] But, writing before the publication of *LALME* and mistaking the dialect, Spearing peremptorily dismissed the suggestion that *Erkenwald* could be the same great poet, 'and indeed it is difficult to understand why the connection was ever made'.[34] Perhaps it might be said, however, that if the four Cotton Nero poems were not all in one manuscript as a sort of 'collected works', there would be more discussion of the single authorship of those poems. In recent years the appreciation of the quality of *Erkenwald* has deepened, so that it is now recognised as a major work, making the possibility of a single author more plausible.

Given that the dialect of *Erkenwald* is no barrier to identity of authorship, it is appropriate to consider the stylistic features the poems share.[35] The vocabulary is drawn from the same pool of poetic words and words of northern dialect, the high-ranking vocabulary for 'man, knight' and so on. Shared with the *Gawain* group alone are such items as the adjective *roynyshe* in *Cleanness* and *Gawain*, and the verbs *nourne*, also in *Cleanness* and *Gawain*, *skelton* in *Cleanness*, and *glew* in the sense 'call', otherwise only in *Patience* 164.[36] The alliterative practice and metrical features of *Erkenwald* are the same as those of the unrhymed poems *Cleanness* and *Patience*: the highly regular aa/ax alliterative pattern, the b-verse rhythms, the syntactical division into quatrains. However, these metrical practices are also features of *Siege* and *Wars*, so that they imply a school of poets, no doubt with much of their work now lost, to include *Wars*, composed further north, and *Siege*, further east. Similarly, the verbal parallels that can seem impressive evidence of single authorship may turn out to be the common currency of a formulaic verse style.[37] For example,

---

[33] Spearing 1970, p. 36.

[34] Spearing 1970, p. 33. The influential essay by Benson 1965 convinced many that the *Gawain* poet did not write *Erkenwald*. Borroff 2006a disagreed, and traced the history of opinion.

[35] For general analysis of vocabulary and style see Borroff 1962, pp. 52–129.

[36] See Oakden 1935, pp. 179–80.

[37] Savage in his edition, pp. lvii–lix, and Oakden 1935, pp. 92–3, list similar phrases and expressions.

an apparently significant parallel is this periphrasis for 'God' in *Erkenwald* and *Cleanness*:

> Toward þe prouidens of þe prince þat paradis weldes
> (*Erkenwald* 161)

> Þat þat ilk proper prynce þat paradys weldez (*Cleanness* 195)

Yet the same periphrasis is found in works that cannot possibly be by the same author:[38]

> If thou haue pleased the prince that paradice weldeth
> (*Death and Liffe* 13)

> Thus he promised to the prince that paradice weldeth
> (*Scottish Field* 88 and 205)

> It es plesynge to the prynce þat paradyse wroghte
> (*Wynnere* 296)

> For to preise the prince that paradise made
> (*Richard the Redeless* I.33)

Further aspects of style and syntax shared by the five poems have been noted, but they do not seem sufficiently distinctive as to advance the argument in favour of unity of authorship.[39]

If shared vocabulary and metre cannot decide the matter, are there other stylistic features, as well as attitudes, preoccupations and agendas, that might help to distinguish the Cotton Nero poems, or alternatively to show that they are shared with *Erkenwald*? Critics have put forward various broad themes that unite the Cotton Nero poems. Most commonly it has been observed that in *Gawain*, *Patience* and *Pearl*, and in episodes in *Cleanness*, the protagonist is confronted by a supernatural power, God or the Green Knight.[40] In these poems humans are often rather comic creatures, and their frailties are treated with an indulgent condescension, except when, as in *Cleanness*, their sinfulness amounts to rebellion. Their struggle and humbling expose

---

[38] See Benson 1965, in particular n. 15.
[39] See Borroff 2006a.
[40] Spearing 1970, p. 32; Burrow 1971, p. 102.

their human weakness, but in the process we come to understand and sympathise with their failure. Our interest is in their flawed character and their motivation. The exemplary judge and the saintly bishop have no such failings; they are admirable for their courage and selflessness, but the interest lies elsewhere, in the unfolding narrative of how such goodness manages to find a solution to the judge's dire situation.

Descriptions in *St Erkenwald* that so vividly give an impression of tactile solidity may certainly be compared to those in the *Gawain* poems, such as the workmen in St Paul's labouring to prise open the tomb lid:

> Putten prises þerto, pinchid one-vnder,
> Kaghten by þe corners with crowes of yrne.
> (*Erkenwald* 69–71)

Such technical detail is even more prominent in the setting sail of Jonah's ship:

> Then he tron on þo tres and þay her tramme ruchen,
> Cachen up þe crossayl, cables þay fasten,
> Wiȝt at þe wyndas weȝen her ankres,
> Spynde spak to þe sprete þe spare bawelyne,
> Gederen to þe gyde-ropes, þe grete cloþ falles.
> (*Patience* 101–05)

[Then he stepped onto those ship-boards and they (the sailors) prepare the tackle, pull up the square sail, fasten cables, quickly weigh their anchors at the windlass, swiftly fasten the spare bowline to the bowsprit, tug at the guide-ropes and the mainsail comes down.]

The architectural detail of the construction of the Heavenly Jerusalem:

> Wyth gentyl gemmez anvnder pyȝt
> Wyth bantelez twelue on basyng boun,
> Þe foundementez twelue of riche tenoun;
> Vch tabelment watz a serlypez ston. (*Pearl* 991–4)

[With fine gems placed underneath, with twelve coursings set at the base, the twelve foundations of splendid construction; each tier was a separate stone.]

finds a parallel in

> Mony a mery mason was made þer to wyrke,
> Harde stones for to hewe with eggite toles,
> Mony grubber in grete þe grounde for to seche
> Þat þe fundement on fyrst shuld þe fote halde.
>
> (*Erkenwald* 39–42)

Sometimes there are even closer parallels, such as the indecipherable writing around the tomb lid and the writing on the wall at Belshazzar's feast (*Cleanness* 1545). Many more examples from all the poems could be cited, yet similarly precise and evocative descriptions may be found in all the best alliterative poems.

A particular characteristic of the *Gawain* poet's descriptive technique is the observation of an object from the perspective of the viewer. As Gawain rides towards the castle, the reader sees the building disclosed as he approaches; so too, as the Dreamer in *Pearl* takes in the view of the Heavenly Jerusalem, we follow his observing eye, first in the general view, then in more detail to the foundations, upwards to the battlements, and then over them into the city that rises above. This sophisticated technique, perhaps learnt from French romance, has no parallel in *Erkenwald*.[41]

Exploring the poets' theology and agenda is perhaps more revealing. For example, no-one comparing the story of the ancient judge with Langland's treatment of the emperor Trajan could possibly suppose that Langland wrote *St Erkenwald*.[42] It is Trajan's *treuth* alone that saves him:

> Troianus was a trewe knyȝte and toke neuere cristendome
> And he is sauf so seith þe boke and his soule in heuene.
>
> (B.12.302–3)

[Trajan was a true knight who never became a Christian, and yet is saved, as the book says, and his soul is in heaven.]

As a pagan in Christian times Trajan had the opportunity to believe, but even so he was saved 'nouȝt þorw preyere of a pope' (B.11.160) but

---

[41] Putter 1995, pp. 31–5; Turville-Petre 2018, pp. 46–7.

[42] For a comparison see Whatley 1986, and, for a rather different view, Grady 1992.

> saued as 3e may se with-oute syngyng of masses
> By loue and by lernyng of my lyuyng in treuthe
> Brou3te me fro bitter peyne þere no biddyng my3te. (B.11.155–7)

[saved as you can see without mass-singing, by love and by learning of my living in truth, which brought me from bitter pain where no prayer could.]

So, too, Erkenwald wrongly supposes the judge, living before the time of Christ, must have been saved by his *ri3t*, 'justice', for good deeds without faith are worthless, as the judge himself points out (301). It is the bishop's baptism alone that redeems the judge and dispatches his soul to bliss. Perhaps the author of *St Erkenwald* composed his poem as a direct rebuttal of the inherent anticlericalism of Langland's account. It may be suggested that there is a vein of anticlerical sentiment running also through the poems of Cotton Nero.[43] From the opening denunciation in *Cleanness* of the wickedness of filthy priests, from the dutiful pointlessness of Gawain's confession to the priest, from Jonah's direct access to God without a priest's intervention, to the complete absence of any clerical figure in *Pearl*, the poet underplays the priestly role in salvation that the author of *St Erkenwald* elevates to a vital principle, presenting his story of the good judge as the extreme case to prove it. Even the judge must call on a bishop to intercede between him and the supreme Judge. Is this the same God who playfully rebukes the disobedient Jonah; who gives Noah instructions on building the Ark; who bargains with Abraham on the number of good people required to save Sodom? All in all, it seems that the evidence is rather against single authorship. It may be that we have to accept that at least two major poets were writing in the same area of Cheshire at much the same time.

4. Sources

The Prologue

The first section of the poem takes us through the early history of the Anglo-Saxons, from their arrival in Britain (c. 450) to the Conversion by Augustine (597) and the episcopate of Erkenwald (675–93). The authorities are Bede's *Ecclesiastical History* and Geoffrey of Monmouth's *History of the Kings of Britain*. Bede describes how the pagan Saxons

---

[43] See Campbell 2018.

led by Hengist and Horsa came to Britain in AD 449: 'The just Judge ordained that the fire of their brutal conquerors should ravage all the neighbouring cities and countryside. ... Public and private buildings fell in ruins; priests were everywhere slain at their altars; prelates and people alike, perished by sword and fire regardless of rank' (Bede i.15). Geoffrey adds: 'Such Britons as remained sought refuge in the western parts of the kingdom: that is, in Cornwall and Wales' (Geoffrey xi.10). Furthermore, Bede remarks, the Britons 'never preached the faith to the Saxons or Angles who inhabited Britain with them' (i.22). Geoffrey puts the blame for the apostasy on the English, 'who, blinded by their pagan beliefs, had completely destroyed Christianity in the part of the island they occupied' (xi.12).

In 597, during the pontificate of Gregory, 'about 150 years after the coming of the Angles to Britain, Gregory, prompted by divine inspiration, sent a servant of God named Augustine, and several more God-fearing monks with him to preach the word of God to the English race' (Bede i.23). They landed on the Isle of Thanet, at that time separated from the mainland of Kent by the Wantsum estuary, as described by Bede (i.25). The poet instead names the landing-place as Sandwich (12), which in his day was one of the cinque ports on the mainland nearby. The missionaries settled in Canterbury and by their preaching converted many of the Kentish people and restored the churches (Bede 1.26):

> Þen prechyd he here þe pure faythe and plantyd þe trouthe,
> And conuertyd all þe communnatés to Cristendame newe.
> (13–14)

The pope wrote to Augustine giving instructions on a number of issues: he was to appoint bishops throughout the country, and it was ordered 'that the idol temples of that race should by no means be destroyed, but only the idols in them. Take holy water and sprinkle it in those shrines, build altars and place relics in them' (Bede i.30). And so Augustine:

> He turnyd temples þat tyme þat temyd to þe devell,
> And clansyd hom in Cristes nome and kyrkes hom callid.
> (15–17)

The pagan gods named by the poet are Apollo, Mahoun, the Sun, Jupiter and Juno. In Geoffrey's account of the mixed heritage of ancient Trojans, Romans and Germanic peoples, the pagan inhabitants of Britain could call upon a varied pantheon of gods.[44] When Vortigern asks Hengist about his religion, he lists the Saxon gods as 'Saturn, Jupiter ... and more, especially Mercury, whom in our language we call Woden. ... Next after him we worship the goddess who is the most powerful of them all, Freia' (Geoffrey vi.11). Earlier Geoffrey had recorded that King Bladud, attempting to fly, crash-landed on the temple of Apollo in London and killed himself (ii.10). The poet's Mahoun, a shortened form of Mahomet, is widely used as the name of a pagan God. In his account of the cleansing of the temples at the first conversion of Britain, Laȝamon, translating Wace, in turn translating Geoffrey, says that the images called Mahun ('þe Mahun weoren ihatene', *Brut* 5079) were taken out and thrown into the fire. Wace (*Roman* 6773-80) and Laȝamon (*Brut* 6937-41) add Phoebus, god of the sun, Jupiter and Apollo (among others) to Hengist's list in Geoffrey. It is odd that the distinctively Saxon deities – Woden and Freia – are not named in *Erkenwald*, though the 'maghty deuel' (27), the 'dryghtyn derrest of ydols praysid' (29), who owned St Paul's itself and whom the poet will not invoke by name, presumably alludes to Woden, the more terrifying for not being identified.

At the time of the conversion, says the poet, London was known as 'þe Newe Troie' (25). On settling in Britain, the Trojan exile Brutus 'built his city and called it Troia Nova. It was known by this name for long ages after, but finally by the corruption of the word it came to be called Trinovantum' (Geoffrey i.17). In fact the Trinovantes were a British tribe identified by Orosius and others. Geoffrey's influential statement held political implications in the late fourteenth century, as when Nicholas Brembre, former mayor of London, was accused of planning to rename the city Parva Troia with himself as duke.[45] St Paul's itself was reckoned 'þe thrid temple ... of þe Triapolitanes' (31). Again this reflects Geoffrey, who reports that at the first conversion the three pagan *archiflamines*, 'high priests', in London, York and Caerleon, were replaced by three archbishops (Geoffrey iv.19).

Bede gives us the few reliable facts we know of Erkenwald's life. He succeeded Mellitus, Cedd and Wini, none of whom is mentioned by the poet, as bishop of the East Saxons in 675, with London as his see. He established two monasteries, one for himself at Chertsey in Surrey, the other for his sister at Barking in Essex. The poet says that the bishop was visiting an abbey in Essex at the time of the discovery

[44] On the imagined heathen gods of the Britons see Gibson 2013, pp. 7-37.
[45] Walsingham, *Historia Anglicana*, ed. Riley, 2.174.

of the tomb (108). He 'lived so holy a life', says Bede, 'that even now miracles bear witness to it', though he mentions just one miracle, that the horse litter which is still preserved cures many sick people (iv.6). The twelfth-century hagiographies, the *Miracula sancti Erkenwaldi* and *Vita Erkenwaldi*, may have been known to the poet, but it is not evident that he used them.[46]

The Discovery of the Tomb

Using crowbars and levers to prise off the heavy lid of the tomb with its mysterious inscription, workmen reveal a body quite untouched by decay and with spotless clothes:

> As wemles were his wedes withouten any tecche
> Oþir of moulyng oþir of motes oþir moght-freten,
> And as bry3t of hor blee in blysnande hewes
> As þai had 3epely in þat 3orde bene 3isturday shapen;
> And als freshe hym þe face and the flesh nakyd
> Bi his eres and bi his hondes þat openly shewid
> With ronke rode as þe rose and two rede lippes,
> As he in sounde sodanly were slippid opon slepe. (85–92)

Such miraculous discoveries, *inventiones*, are an established hagiographic genre, and proclaim, ironically as it turns out, that this is the body of a saint.[47] The poet would have known Bede's description of the disinterred remains of St Cuthbert:

> Opening the grave they found the body intact and whole as if it were still alive, the joints of the limbs flexible, and much more like a sleeping than a dead man. Moreover all his garments in which the limbs had been clothed were not only undefiled but seemed to be perfectly new and wonderfully bright. (iv. 30).

Another example from Bede concerns Etheldreda, abbess of Ely, who died of cancer of the jaw. Sixteen years later, Bede reports, the new abbess sent brethren to find material for a more magnificent

---

[46] Gordon Whatley notes a loose parallel with an episode from the *Vita* used in the liturgy of the saint; see Whatley 1982, 282–3. For texts and translations see Whatley 1989.

[47] Otter 1994, 390–6, and Otter 1996. Whatley 1982, 286–90, finds 'definite links' between the poem and the legend of the Invention of the Holy Cross.

tomb, 'a coffin beautifully made of white marble'. When they opened Etheldreda's coffin they discovered the tumour had healed, the body was 'as uncorrupt as if she had died and been buried that very day', and the linen cloths were 'as whole and fresh as on the very day when they had been put around her chaste limbs' (iv.19).

Matthew Paris (d. 1259), the chronicler of St Alban's Abbey, records several accounts of the protomartyr St Alban.[48] In his *Vie de seint Auban* in Anglo-Norman verse in Trinity Dublin MS 177 Matthew recounts how King Offa in 792 directed workmen to dig with their spades and their picks until they came across the bones of the saint. The lively illustration on f. 59r shows the navvies at work and a bishop holding up Alban's severed skull. Offa then constructs the church and Alban's remains are honourably reburied. Matthew describes the rediscovery of the tomb in 1257 in terms comparable to the description of the excavation of Erkenwald's coffin. Repairs are being made to the east end of St Alban's church, where a wall is collapsing:

> Whilst the mason's labourers were working with their spades on the pavement, they fancied, from the ringing sound of their tools and the noise of their footsteps, that something unusual and unknown of was hidden under them. On examining deeper down, they found under the earth, though not very deep, a stone tomb, in a spot between the altar of St Oswin, where morning mass was usually performed, and the altar of St Wulstan, where was also placed an antique painted bier and a tomb of marble with marble pillars also, and this was said to be the ancient tomb and burial place of St Alban. ... In this tomb also was found a leaf of lead, on which, according to the custom of the ancients, was cut the following inscription: 'In this tomb was found the venerable body of St Alban, the chief martyr of England.'[49]

Such *inventiones* were, of course, designed to enhance the status of the church involved.

---

[48] See McCulloch 1981. Otter 1994, 391–9, makes the comparison with *St Erkenwald*.
[49] Matthew Paris, *Chronica Majora*, 3.213.

The Pagan Judge

Though there is no direct source for the story of the pagan judge, there are parallels with the very popular legend of Trajan.[50] In the earliest version of the legend, from the early eighth century, St Gregory (pope 590–604) was crossing the Forum of Trajan (Roman emperor AD 98–117) where he learnt of Trajan's kindness to a widow in arranging restitution for the death of her son.[51] Gregory wept with compassion for Trajan, who had died a pagan, and was assured by a divine revelation that his prayers had been answered and that Trajan had been baptised by his tears. This Latin account, written by a monk from the Northumbrian monastery at Whitby, survives in just one continental manuscript from the ninth century. Writing in Rome in the late ninth century, John the Deacon's *Vita Sancti Gregorii* refers to the Whitby life 'quod apud Saxones legitur', and through his version the legend spread widely.[52] By the later Middle Ages the Trajan story had proliferated in different guises to serve different ends. It featured as an episode in the life of St Gregory in Jacobus de Voragine's *Legenda Aurea*; Ranulf Higden's *Polychronicon* gave a historical account; Dante singled out Trajan for his justice in the *Commedia*, in both the *Purgatorio* and the *Paradiso*, and in *Piers Plowman* Langland offered an idiosyncratic take on the story. The crucial difference between the Trajan legend and *St Erkenwald* is that Trajan, as a pagan who lived during the Christian era, had the opportunity to learn of Christ, an opportunity denied to the ancient judge.

The points of contact between the *miraculum* of St Erkenwald and that of St Gregory are that a just man who has died a pagan is saved through the prayers of a saint. A version of the legend that includes the discovery of the tomb is provided by *Fiori di filosofi* (1270s) once attributed to Brunetto Latini.[53] In this, learning of Trajan's kindness towards the widow, Gregory opened Trajan's tomb, where he found a skull containing a living tongue, 'sana e fresca come d'uomo vivo' ['healthy and fresh as a living man'], preserved because Trajan's words had always been just. Gregory wept and begged God that Trajan might be released from hell. 'And this Emperor Trajan was freed from the pains of hell and went to heaven for his justice and for the pleas of St Gregory the pope.' However, because he had prayed for something so irregular, Gregory was punished by sickness for the rest of his life. This version of

---

[50] For a full account of the legend see Whatley 1984a.
[51] *Earliest Life of Gregory the Great*, pp. 126–9; see Whatley 1984a, 27–8.
[52] Quoted O'Loughlin and Conrad-O'Briain 1993, 67.
[53] *Fiore di filosofi*, ed. Cappelli, pp. 58–61.

the legend was depicted in a series of paintings by Roger van der Weyden in about 1440 for the town hall in Brussels, reproduced a few years later in a tapestry before being destroyed in the seventeenth century, showing Trajan and the distressed widow, Gregory praying and then worshipping the skull and tongue.[54] The Latin beneath the panel explains that the tongue was preserved on account of the justice which it had pronounced.

Even closer to *St Erkenwald* is the related version of the story, also in Italian, by Jacopo della Lana (1324–8), an early commentator on the *Commedia*, commenting on Dante's reference to Trajan in the *Purgatorio* 10.73–8.[55] In this account workmen digging the foundations for a building in Rome excavated an ancient sarcophagus. On opening it they found among the bones a skull containing a tongue 'cosi rigida, carnosa e fresca' ['as stiff, fleshy and fresh'] as if it had just been buried. This was regarded as a great marvel in view of its age. The news reached Gregory, and, having ordered the remains to be brought to him, he conjured the corpse in God's name to identify itself. The tongue revealed that it was the emperor Trajan, who had been a ruler in Christian times and was condemned to hell for lack of faith. When the records were examined, they showed that Trajan had been a man of mercy and justice, as when he handed his own son over to avenge the murder of the widow's son. On learning of this story, Gregory was moved to pray for Trajan, who was restored to life and was baptised. However, because Gregory had prayed for a damned man, he suffered from 'male di stomaco' for the rest of his life.

In some respects the closest analogue of all is a story in Werner Rolevinck's *De laude antiquae Saxonicae nunc Westphaliae dictae*, printed in Cologne in about 1474.[56] Instead of Trajan and Gregory, this involves an unnamed judge and the bishop of Vienna. The event takes place in Vienna in the year 1200, when a corpse was discovered with the tongue and lips intact. In answer to the archbishop's enquiry, the corpse replies: 'I was a pagan and judge in this place, and my tongue never uttered a false judgement, therefore I cannot die until I've been born again by the water of baptism and have ascended to heaven.'[57] The

---

[54] For a reproduction see OnlineWeb Gallery of Art.

[55] Text from dantelab.dartmouth.edu/reader.

[56] Rolevinck, *De laude*, ed. Bücher, p. 26. This extract is printed in Gollancz's *St Erkenwald*, p. 55.

[57] 'Ego eram paganus et iudex in hoc loco, nec unquam lingua mea protulit iniquam sententiam quare etiam mori non possum, donec aqua baptismi renatus ad coelum evolvem'.

head was duly baptised and immediately the tongue crumbled into dust. In the same passage Rolevinck records another widespread legend of an ancient tomb on which was inscribed in gold the statement that the enclosed corpse had believed that Christ would be born of the Virgin, thus supporting the notion of intuitive or implicit faith.[58]

Rolevinck's account shows how widespread different versions of the Trajan legend were throughout the Middle Ages, matching *Erkenwald* to a greater or lesser extent and with different details, and demonstrates how the legend could be used to support different agendas. The earliest version, the Whitby Life, stresses the necessity for baptism: 'The soul of the Emperor Trajan was refreshed and even baptised by Gregory's tears.' The author continues with a puzzling statement: 'Let no-one be surprised that we say he was baptised, for without baptism none will ever see God; and a third kind of baptism is by tears [nemo enim sine babtismo Deum videbit umquam: cuius tertium genus est lacrime].'[59] Whatever this means, it is not analogous to *St Erkenwald*, since Trajan is not resurrected and Gregory's sorrowful tears do not fall on his body. In fact it seems to be the writer's over-literal interpretation of a metaphor referring to the tears of a penitent throughout life, and not to the sacrament of baptism.[60] All reference to such an unorthodox baptism is dropped in John the Deacon's rewriting of the legend, who concludes that, since Trajan was not baptised, Gregory's tears could do no more than lessen his punishments in hell. Trajan's baptism is also mentioned in della Lana and Rolevinck, but 'neither in della Lana nor any other version of the Gregory/Trajan story does it form the narrative climax and centerpiece'.[61] In most of the other accounts Trajan is not baptised.

The judge buried in St Paul's lived before Christ with no opportunity to know Christ's teaching and receive baptism. Theologians juggled with the notion of redemption through implicit faith in such cases, but Trajan, a Roman alive in Christian times, had every opportunity, which leads to questions about how or whether he was redeemed. In Langland's interpretation Trajan was neither resuscitated or baptised, but 'was broken oute of helle' on account of 'his pure treuthe'. Gregory

---

[58] For the history of this legend see Whatley 1986, 346–8.
[59] *Earliest Life of Gregory the Great*, pp. 126–7.
[60] See O'Loughlin and Conrad-O'Briain 1993. Duffy 2018, pp. 176–81, draws out the parallels with the Whitby *Earliest Life of Gregory the Great*, but accepts the poet is most unlikely to have known it.
[61] Whatley 1986, 358.

wept for him, Trajan explains, wishing that he might merit grace and be saved. As a result the pagan emperor was released from the bitter pain of hell for his 'lyuyng in treuthe' (*Piers Plowman* B.11.156). As 'a trewe kny3t', even though he 'toke neuere cristendome', yet 'he is sauf, so seith þe boke, and his soule is in heuene' (*Piers Plowman* B.12.302-03). This is in sharp contrast to *St Erkenwald*, in which the response to ideas expressed by those such as Langland magnifies the role of the bishop just as Langland minimised the role of the pope.[62]

5. Theology: Heaven and Hell

Pagan Salvation
No other version of the legend of the revived pagan shares *St Erkenwald*'s emphasis on religious ceremony and ritual. There is no parallel to Erkenwald's surprising decision not to examine the body that he has been summoned back to see, but instead to prepare for the encounter by spending the night praying for divine guidance, and to begin the next day attired in his pontifical vestments celebrating a sung high mass. When he processes through the cathedral to the corpse, the nobles bow to him respectfully, in recognition of his clerical eminence and his leadership of the citizens in a time of agitation and turbulence. His dialogue with the body takes place in an ecclesiastical setting after he has been divinely inspired through prayer. The orthodoxy is firmly maintained, and it is in this context that the surprising baptism takes place.[63] Though the performance of the sacrament might be described as minimalist, the formal requirements, the water and the words, are present.

St Erkenwald propounds a notably conservative view in an age when the position of the Church, its wealth and its panoply of rituals, were coming under attack, both from those who criticised its corruption and from those who questioned its doctrines. The more radical critics, notably Wycliffe and the Lollards, were beginning to question the very nature and value of the sacraments and the priesthood, and in *Piers Plowman* Langland raises related issues.[64] Yet for the author of *St Erkenwald* there is no salvation without baptism.

An often-cited maxim from the Office for the Dead is '*Quia in inferno nulla est redempcio*/"For in hell", he says, "Es na redempcyoune"'

---

[62] Grady 1992; Whatley 1986, 333.
[63] See Kamowski 1995.
[64] For a useful overview see Adams 1988. On the theology of *St Erkenwald* see Whatley 1986, esp. 342-5; Kamowski 1995. For an alternative reading, Sisk 2007.

(*Prick of Conscience* 7245–6). The damned are condemned to pain everlasting. This truth was a severe embarrassment to theologians trying to interpret the story of Trajan's release from hell as a reward for his good deeds. Various unsatisfactory solutions were proposed. In the words of *Gilte Legende*, a translation of Jacobus de Voragine's life of Gregory in *Legenda Aurea*:[65]

> Some sayn that Troian was repeled ayein to lyff and hadde grace for to deserue foryeuenesse, and so he hadde euerlasting ioye and he was not fynably ordeined to be dampned in helle by sentence diffinitif. And some other sayen that the soule of Troian was not symply assoiled from euerlasting payne, but his payne was suspended vnto the day of dome …. etc. (45.352–7)

> [Some say that Trajan was recalled to life and had the grace to deserve forgiveness, and so he had joy everlasting and was not finally ordained to be damned in hell by a decisive sentence. And others say that Trajan's soul was not absolutely absolved from everlasting suffering but his suffering was suspended until Judgement Day.]

Others reported that God punished Gregory severely for praying for a condemned man:

> For thou hast praied for a dampned saule chese one of two thingges: either thou shalt be two dayes in purgatori, or elles all the dayes of thi lyff thou shalt be laboured with continuel languoures and siknesse. (45.372–5)

> [Because you have prayed for a damned soul choose one of two things: either you will spend two days in Purgatory, or else all the days of your life you will be burdened with continual infirmities and sickness.]

The saint chose the latter and consequently was 'either tormented withe potagre [gout], either that he was gretly greued withe other gret sorughes and diseses, or tormented in the stomake mervelously' (45.378–80). Aquinas was perplexed by the case, supposing at one time that God, with foreknowledge that Trajan was to be restored to life by

---

[65] *Gilte Legende*, ed. Hamer 2006. The issues are discussed by Grady 1992.

prayers of a saint, pardoned him; at another time that his punishment was temporarily suspended until Judgement Day.[66]

We have seen that Trajan's case was particularly difficult because, as a pagan in the Christian era, he had the opportunity to believe.[67] In contrast, living long before Christ, the judge in *St Erkenwald* had no such opportunity. The destination of someone in the judge's position, a pagan with good works but with no access to knowledge of Christ, was a subject of much theological speculation. Scripture seems definite on the matter, for Christ said 'no man cometh to the father but by me' (John 14.6), and 'Unless a man be born again of water and the Holy Ghost, he cannot enter into the kingdom of God' (John 3.5). Dante wrestled with the question, and the figure 'Dante' is reproved by the Eagle, representing God's justice, for questioning divine judgement:

> chè tu dicevi: 'Un uom nasce alla riva
>   dell' Indo, e quivi non è chi ragioni
>   di Cristo nè chi legga nè chi scriva;
> e tutti suoi voleri e atti boni
>   sono, quanto ragione umana vede,
>   sanza peccato in vita od in sermoni.
> Muore non battezzato e sanza fede:
>   ov'è questa giustizia che 'l condanna?
>   ov'è la colpa sua, se ei non crede?' (*Paradiso* 19.70–8)

[For thou saidst: 'A man is born on the bank of the Indus, and none is there to speak, or read, or write of Christ, and all his desires and doings are good, so far as human reason sees, without sin in life or speech. He dies unbaptised and without faith. Where is this justice that condemns him? Where is his fault if he does not believe?'][68]

Similarly, Erkenwald assumes that the just judge must have been redeemed:

---

[66] 'Eius poena fuit suspensa ad tempus, sicilet usque ad diem iudicii'; Aquinas, *Commentary on the Sentences* I, d. 43, q. 2, a. 2; *Summa Theologiae* III, suppl. q. 71, a. 5, reply obj. 5. Quotations and translations of *Sentences* and *Summa* are from Aquinas Institute's online texts: aquinasinstitute.org/aquinas-opera-omnia.

[67] An essential study of the developing opinions on the salvation of non-believers is Marenbon 2015b.

[68] Text and translation from *Dante: The Divine Comedy*, ed. Sinclair 1948.

> '3ea, bot sayes þou of þi saule,' þen sayde þe bisshop;
> 'Quere is ho stablid and stadde, if þou so stre3t wro3htes?
> He þat rewardes vche a renke as he has ri3t seruyd
> My3t euel forgo the to gyfe of his grace summe brawnche.
> For as he says in his sothe psalmyde writtes:
> "Þe skilfulle and þe vnskathely skelton ay to me."
> Forþi say me of þi soule, in sele quere ho wonnes,
> And of þe riche restorment þat ra3t hyr oure Lorde.' (273–80)

The bishop bases his belief on the teachings of Thomas Aquinas, who thought about the question deeply and discussed it at length. He answered it with this proposal:

> It pertains to divine providence to furnish everyone with what is necessary for salvation, provided that on his part there is no hindrance. Thus, if someone so brought up followed the direction of natural reason in seeking good and avoiding evil, we must most certainly hold that God would either reveal to him through internal inspiration what had to be believed, or would send some preacher of the faith to him.[69]

Furthermore, Aquinas embraced the idea that pagans could be saved through implicit faith:

> The Gentiles were not established as teachers of divine faith. Hence, no matter how well versed they were in secular wisdom, they should be counted as ordinary people. Therefore, it was enough for them to have implicit faith in the Redeemer, either as part of their belief in the faith of the law and the prophets, or as part of their belief in divine providence itself.[70]

In the case of those who were not baptised because they had no knowledge of Christ, Aquinas outlined the concept of three kinds of baptism:

> Baptism of Water has its efficacy from Christ's Passion, to which a man is conformed by Baptism, and also from the Holy Spirit, as first cause. Now although the effect depends

---

[69] Aquinas, *Quaestiones Disputatae, de Veritate*, q. 14, a. 11; quoted from Isidore. co/aquinas.

[70] Ibid., q. 14, a. 11, answers to difficulties 5.

on the first cause, the cause far surpasses the effect, nor does it depend on it. Consequently, a man may, without Baptism of Water, receive the sacramental effect from Christ's Passion, in so far as he is conformed to Christ by suffering for Him. ... In like manner a man receives the effect of Baptism by the power of the Holy Spirit, not only without Baptism of Water, but also without Baptism of Blood: forasmuch as his heart is moved by the Holy Spirit to believe in and love God and to repent of his sins: wherefore this is also called Baptism of Repentance.[71]

If Baptism of Water was not essential, the judge would have been saved for his good works without Erkenwald's intervention. But alas, he recognises that his good deeds are of no value without faith:

> Quat wan we with oure wele-dede, þat wroghtyn ay riȝt,
> Quen we are dampnyd dulfully into þe depe lake
> And exilid fro þat soper so, þat solempne fest
> Þer richely hit arne refetyd þat after right hungride? (301–04)

This reflects the stern view of Augustine in which pagan virtue is false virtue, and so is of no salvific value.[72] We are all condemned by the sin of 'Adam oure alder þat ete of þat appull' (295), and to atone for original sin it is necessary to receive 'fulloght in fonte with faitheful bileue' (299). Only through some miraculous intervention can the judge receive baptism and be saved.

Hell

Unlike Trajan, however, the judge is not in the hell of the damned but in limbo.[73] In this way the poet avoids the unorthodoxy of a rescue from everlasting punishment, but he escapes that theological trap only to fall into another. There were four possible destinations after death:

> It should be said that hell has four parts. One is the hell of the damned ['infernus damnatorum'], in which there is darkness – both with respect to the lack of the divine vision and with respect to the lack of charity – and there is also a

---

[71] Aquinas, *Summa Theologiae* III, q. 66, a. 11.
[72] See Marenbon 2015b, pp. 32–41, citing Augustine, *Contra Julianum* in particular.
[73] For a fuller account see Turville-Petre 2023a.

sensible punishment there; and this hell is the place of the damned. Another is the hell above this one, in which there is darkness – both on account of the lack of the divine vision and on account of the lack of grace – but there is no sensible punishment there; and this is called the limbo of the children ['limbus puerorum']. There is another above this, in which there is the darkness as regards the lack of the divine vision, but not as regards the lack of grace, but there is a punishment of the senses there; this is called purgatory ['purgatorium']. And there is another yet above this, in which there is the darkness as regards the lack of the divine vision, but not as regards the lack of grace, nor is there a sensible punishment; and this is the hell of the holy patriarchs ['infernus sanctorum patrum']. And Christ descended into this one only, as regards place, but not as regards the experience of darkness.[74]

It is in this last place, to which Christ descended at the harrowing of hell, the 'limbus patrum', that the judge's soul remains in darkness:

> I was non of þe nommbre þat þou with noy boghtes,
> With þe blode of thi body vpon þe blo rode;
> Quen þou herghdes helle-hole and hentes hom þeroute,
> Þi loffynge oute of limbo, þou laftes me þer.
> And þer sittes my soule þat se may no fyrre. (289–93)

There is one problem with this, which is that Christ led out *all* those in the limbo of the patriarchs. Aquinas is firm: 'This hell should now be empty, since after that time no one descends to that limbo.'[75] The author of *The Prick of Conscience* is entirely orthodox on this point, following Aquinas in the fourfold division of hell and describing the *limbus patrum* as a place now quite empty of inhabitants:

> Þat Crist visited when he was dede,
> And þa þat þar war with hym oute tuke
> And left nane þaryn, als says þe buke.
> Ne fra þat tyme, als we here clerkes telle,
> Com never nane yhit þheder to duelle,
> Ne never nane forthward sal com;

---

[74] See Aquinas, *Sentences* III, d. 22, q. 2, a. 1, response to qcla. 2.
[75] Aquinas, *Sentences* III, d. 22, q. 2, a. 2, response to q. 1.

> And þat stede men calles *lymbus patrum*,
> Þe whilk 'a fre preson' on Inglys es
> Whare þe haly faders duelled in myrknes. (2807–15)⁷⁶

[(A place) that Christ visited when he was dead, and took out those who were there with him and left none in there, as the book says. And from that time, as we hear clerics relate, no-one ever came to reside there, and no-one will come in future. And that place is called *Limbo of the Fathers*, which is 'a free prison' in English, where the holy fathers lived in darkness.]

Yet the author of *St Erkenwald* is not the only poet to imagine a limbo peopled by virtuous pagans who lived before Christ. In the fourth canto of the *Inferno*, at the outer circle around Hell, Virgil and Dante reach the limbo of those who had died unbaptised but sinless, both children and adults.⁷⁷ Virgil tells Dante:

> Or vo' che sappi, innanzi che più andi,
> ch'ei non peccaro; e s'elli hanno mercedi,
>   non basta, perchè non ebber battesmo,
> ch' è porta della fede che tu credi.
> E se furon dinanzi al cristianesmo,
>   non adorar debitamente a Dio:
> e di questi cotai son io medesmo. (*Inferno* 4.33–9)

[I would have thee know, then, before thou goest farther, that they did not sin; but though they have merits it is not enough, for they had not baptism, which is the gateway of the faith thou holdest; and if they were before Christianity they did not worship God aright, and of these I am one.]

Dante's guide, Virgil, who died before the birth of Christ, says he had witnessed Christ's descent to rescue the patriarchs, 'quando ci vidi venire un possente, / con segno di vittoria coronato' (4.33–4), 'when I saw a mighty one come here, crowned with a sign of victory', and later he explains to Dante that he forfeited Heaven because he lacked

---

⁷⁶ *The Prick of Conscience*, ed. Hanna and Wood.
⁷⁷ Valuable studies are: Padoan 1969, Iannucci 2005, Marenbon 2015a. Scattergood 2017, pp. 352–4, also compares the treatment of limbo in the *Commedia* and *St Erkenwald*.

faith and for no other fault (*Purgatorio* 7.7–8). Those whom Dante first meets in limbo are the souls of Homer, Horace, Ovid and Lucan: 'sembianza avean nè trista nè lieta' ('their looks were neither sad nor joyful') (*Inferno* 4.84). Together they stroll to a verdant meadow and to an open space 'luminoso e alto' (4.116) where they can observe the other inhabitants, the heroes, philosophers and scholars of antiquity. The inhabitants will be here for eternity and, although they do not suffer physical torment, Virgil says, 'sanza speme vivemo in disio' ('without hope we live in desire') (4.42).

Augustine had explicitly denied that there was a place between heaven and hell, accusing Julian the Pelagian of creating somewhere between damnation and the heavenly kingdom for the ancients who died unbaptised.[78] Dante's early commentators, indeed, remarked on the unorthodoxy of his picture of limbo. Guido da Pisa (c. 1328), commenting on canto 4.82–4, censured Dante: 'Nostra fides non tenet quod ibi non sint nisi parvuli innocentes. Iste autem poeta in hac parte, et in quibusdam aliis, loquitur non theologice sed poetice' ['Our faith does not hold that there are here any other than innocent children. Here and in certain other places the poet speaks not theologically but poetically'].[79] In the mid-fifteenth century St Antoninus, archbishop of Florence, was even more forthright in his condemnation, accusing Dante of leading his readers into error by conjuring up 'antiquos sapientes … in Campis Elysiis' ['the wise men of old in the Elysian fields'].[80]

Christ himself said: 'He that believeth and is baptised shall be saved, but he that believeth not shall be condemned' (Mark 16.16). For the *Erkenwald* poet, as for Dante, faith and baptism are necessary for salvation; yet this leaves them in a quandary because of their admiration for the virtues of righteous pagans and the conviction that they could not have been condemned to eternal suffering. And so the judge as 'a freke faitheles' (287) has been held back in limbo, remaining in suspended animation through a 'goste-lyfe' granted by God (192), waiting for the miracle of the inadvertent baptism by the bishop's tears that will release him. Neither the *Erkenwald* poet nor Dante is writing

---

[78] 'Provisuri estis aliquem locum inter damnationem regnumque coelorum, ubi non sint in miseria sed in beatitudine sempiterna', Augustine, *Contra Julianum* 4.3.26.

[79] Guido da Pisa in dantelab.dartmouth.edu/reader. Of Dante's limbo Marenbom remarks that 'the extra role it is given, as home for the virtuous pagans, is his innovation' (2015b, p. 208).

[80] This is quoted by Padoan 1969, 379, and Iannucci 2005, p. 72.

a theological tract, and what is theologically untenable works poetically in exposing the difficulty in coming to terms with the conflicting demands of faith and justice.

6. Language and Vocabulary

There is secure evidence for locating the ownership of MS Harley 2250 in Cheshire and south Lancashire in the early sixteenth century, and *LALME* places the scribal dialects of the English texts firmly in Cheshire, with the dialect of *St Erkenwald* located in south-east Cheshire. The fact that *LALME*'s listing of forms in *St Erkenwald* in LP 419 is not fully accurate does not alter this conclusion.[81] Whether the scribal forms differed from the authorial dialect is impossible to determine in the absence of evidence from rhymes, though the first line of the poem indicates that the author was also from Cheshire. The fact that the text has comparatively few errors and misunderstandings perhaps implies that there were not many copies between author and scribe.

Spellings and Sounds
Vowels
Significant for determining dialect are the following:
The reflex of OE and ON /a/ before a nasal not lengthened usually appears as *o*: *bonkes* 32, *con* 156, *mon* 97, *mony* 11, *nome* 16, but *name* 18 (*LALME* dot maps 91, 95, 837, 839).

OE and ON /a/ when lengthened before a nasal or /l/ is usually *o* but sometimes *a*: *honde* 84, *londe* 200, *long* 1, *ronge* 117, *wrang* 236, *colde* 305, *holde* 249, *halde* 42; *LALME* dot maps 930–1, 936–7.

OE and ON /a:/ appears as *o*: *bones* 346, *fro* 12, *holy* 127, *home* 107. Cf. *LALME* dot maps 633, 852.

OE /a:/ + /w/ usually appears as *ou/ow*, but occasionally *au/aw*: *soule* 279, but *saule* 273, *knowe* 74, but *vnknawen* 147; *LALME* dot maps 887, 888, 813, 815.

'Eyes' and 'high' (OE *ēagan* and *hēh*) are *eghen* 194 and *hegh* 137; in the *Gawain* ms. *yȝen* and *hyȝe*; *LALME* dot maps 753–4, 437. Adj. 'own' (OE

---

[81] E.g. *are* not *ar*; *were* not *wer*; HAVE pl. add *has*, *haue*. The lists of forms of pr. 3 sg. and pl., weak pa. t. sg. and pl., weak and strong pp. should all be expanded as in 'Verbs' below.

āgen) is *awen* 235, varying with *owen* in the *Gawain* ms.; *LALME* dot maps 497–8.

'Each' (OE *ǣlc*) is *vche* 204, *LALME* dot map 89; 'each one' is *vschon* 93. 'Think' (OE *þencan*) is *thenke* 225, *LALME* dot map 299. 'Through' (OE *þurh*) is *thurgh* 123, *LALME* vol. 4.98; 'though' is *þagh* 122 (OE *þēah*), and once *þof* 320 (ON *þó*); *LALME* dot maps 198, 203, vol. 4.58.

Consonants
OE /hw/ is *qu-* (once *qw-*: *qwo* 185): *quat* 54, *quen* 57, *quy* 186, *LALME* dot map 270. In this last case *quy* alliterates with *worlde* and *weghe*, a practice shared with the *Gawain* poems. For OE /ʃ/ the spelling is usually *sh-*: *shal* 174, *sheddes* 329, *shewid* 90, but twice *sch-*: *schedde* 182, *schewyd* 180, *LALME* dot maps 144–5.

Inflexions
Nouns
For metrical purposes the poet may retain final *-e* on nouns and adjectives when historically justified, a practice not consistently observed by the scribe. See below under Metre. The plural ends in *-es* (but *questis* 133). Nouns of French origin ending in *-l*, *-r* or *-n* regularly drop the *e*: *bedels* 59, *corners* 71, *ydols* 17, *resons* 164, but *bordures* 82. Pl. 'eyes' is *eghen* 311; 'years' and 'winters' have no ending after a numeral, *ȝere* 208, *wynter* 230. The gen. sg. also ends in *-es*, though *fader* 243 has no ending.

Personal Pronouns
The 3 pl. forms for 'she, her' are *ho, hyr*; for 'they, them, their' are *þai, hom, hor*. See *LALME* dot maps 11, 21, 24, 31, 48, 61.

Verbs
Infinitive: Without ending or with *-e*: *amounte* 284, *blynne* 111, *bogh* 194, *bryng* 56.

Present Indicative: 1 sg. regularly *-e*: *hope* 4, *knowe* 263, *folwe* 318. 2 sg. *-(e)s*: *has* 187, *says* 159, *sheddes* 329. 3 sg. *-(e)s*: *biddes* 221, *has* 147, *rewardes* 275, *says* 277, but *bashis* 261. *LALME* dot map 645. Pl. is as often the northern *-(e)s* as the midland *-en/-on*: *has* 148, *heldes* 196, *leues* 176, *longen* 268, *repairen* 135, *skelton* 278, *soupen* 336; without ending *se* 170. *LALME* dot maps 652–3.

Past Indicative Strong Verbs: 1 & 3 sg. end *-e*: *bede* 243, *toke* 313, *come* 113, *ete* 295, *shope* 129. 2 sg. usually has *-es*: *laftes* 292, *wroghtes* 274, sometimes -e: *werpe* 329. Pl. has -e(n): *bete* 9, *cladden* 249, *commen* 63, *dalfe* 45, sometimes no ending: *wan* 301 (with the vowel of the sg.).

Past Indicative Weak verbs: 1 & 3 sg. ending -ed/-et/-yd/-yt: *deghed* 246, *brayed* 190, *declynet* 237, *askyd* 96, *conuertyd* 14, *heldyt* 137. 2 sg. ending -es: *hades* 224, *hentes* 291, *herghdes* 291. Pl. ending: -ed(e)/-de(n)/-(e)t/-yd/-yt: *auisyd* 53, *beryd* 352, *hungride* 304, *besiet* 56, *boghit* 59, *laide* 72, *listonde* 219, *muset* 54, *couert* 346, *gurden* 251, *haden* 8. LALME dot map 655.

Subjunctive: without ending or -e: 3 sg.: *digne* 123, *fulsen* 124, *lene* 315, *se* 308. For 'be', pr. 1 sg. *be* 122, 3 sg. *be* 324, pa. 3 sg. *were* 72.

Imperative: sg. -e: *be* 181, *biknowe* 220, *councele* 184.

Present Participle: Always -and(e): *blysnande* 87, *dwynande* 294, *wepand* 122, LALME dot map 346.

Past Participle: Strong verbs usually have -(e)n/-on/-yn: *beten* 37, *bitan* 28, *shapen* 88, *walon* 64, *worthyn* 330, but the ending is sometimes lost: *kest* 83, *putte* 153, LALME dot maps 663–4. Weak verbs have -ed(e)/-de/-yd/-yt: *araide* 77, *arayed* 271, *bende* 182, *breuyt* 103, *iuggit* 180, *iuggid* 188, LALME dot maps 658–9.

For forms of preterite-present verbs see Glossary s.v. *aghtes, con, may, shal, thar, wost*.

Such differences as there are between the scribal dialects of *St Erkenwald* and the four *Gawain* poems are accounted for by the gap of three-quarters of a century between Cotton Nero A.x and Harley 2250.[82] There is no evidence to determine whether the authorial language differed.

Vocabulary
Erkenwald shares the traditional alliterative vocabulary of other north-west midland poems, especially the *Gawain* group.[83] Thus poetic words for 'man' – *freke* (287, 323), *haþel* (198), *lede* (4×), *renke* (275),

---

[82] The language of the *Gawain* poems is analysed in the edition of *Sir Gawain and the Green Knight* by Tolkien, Gordon and Davis (1967), and more fully by Serjeantson in the edition by Gollancz (1940). *LALME* lists the forms of the *Gawain* poems as LP 26, mapped as east Cheshire on the border with Staffordshire. For a critique and correction of *LALME*'s listing see Putter and Stokes (2007), though they agree on this location.

[83] See Borroff 1962, 27–129.

segge (6×), *tulkes* (109), *weghe* (73, 96, 186) – are shared with the *Gawain* poems, though *burne*, *gome* and *schalk* do not appear in *Erkenwald*. Shared with the *Gawain* group alone are *nourne* v. (101, 152, 195), in *Cleanness* (3×), *Gawain* (5×); *skelton* v. (278), in *Cleanness* (4×); *roynyshe* adj. (52), in *Cleanness* (1545) and *Gawain* (457); *glew* v. (171) in the sense 'call' otherwise only in *Patience* 164. Idealising adjectives such as *hende*, *reken* and *ronke* are frequent.

The more technical vocabulary reflects the range and detail of descriptions, mainly in the first half of the poem. Building and architectural terms for the excavation and the tomb itself are *mason*, *grubber*, *fundement*, *throgh*, *gargeles*, *sperl*, *spelunke*, *planed*, *prises*, *crowes* and later *cloyster*. The body is dressed in a *gowne* with a *gurdill*, a *mantel* furred with *menyuer*, fabric of *camelyn* with fine *bordures* and on the head a *coyfe*. Londoners are not named but identified by office: *burgeys*, *bedels*, *maire*, *sextene*, *dene*. Given the subject, legal and religious terms are perhaps less common than might be supposed. *Title* (28) is used in a legal sense, and the terms *sayd causes* (202) and *sesyd in* (345) are specifically legal. Religious expressions are *relaide*, 'apostate' (11) and *cenacle* (336) from the Vulgate. If the interpretation offered here is correct, *loffynge* (292) is a calque on the Vulgate *reliquae*. Equally inventive is, perhaps, *triapolitan* (31, 36), apparently the poet's coinage based on *metropolitan*.

7. Metre

Alliteration and the Structure of the Line

The standard alliterative line has two lifts or beats in the a-verse alliterating with the first of two lifts in the b-verse. This pattern is represented as aa/ax, with 'x' denoting the final non-alliterating lift:

>   Ther was a **b**yschop in þat **b**urgh   **b**lessyd and sacryd (3)

Less obviously:

>   **A**nsuare here to my sawe   councele no trouthe (184)

Vowels alliterate with other vowels and /h/ (90), and some consonant clusters alliterate with themselves (/kl/ 140, /sk/ 278, /sl/ 331, /sp/ 335, /st/ 219); /s/ also alliterates with /ʃ/ (129) and /sl/ (92); /kw/ (spelt *qu*) alliterates with /k/ in l. 74, and with /w/ in lines 185–6.

The basic scheme can be enriched. There may be three alliterating syllables in the a-verse:

> He turnyd temples þat tyme   þat temyd to þe deuell (15)

In addition, the last lift may alliterate:

> The bolde Breton Sir Belyn   Sir Berynge was his brothire (213)

Whether there are three lifts in an 'extended' a-verse or the regular pattern with two lifts dominates so that one is subordinated is a matter of debate.[84] In favour of two lifts there are lines of the same shape except that the third possible lift does not alliterate and is more readily subordinated (aa(x)/ax):

> þe mecul mynster þerinne   a maghty deuel aghte (27; cf. 59, 70)

> And chaungit cheuely hor nomes   and chargit hom better (18)

In many alliterative poems the aa/ax pattern is a condition of metricality, so that a divergence from the pattern indicates corruption.[85] With poems preserved in a single manuscript the evidence is less secure, but it is likely to be the case in *Erkenwald*. Very few lines do not conform to the standard basic pattern. One line lacks alliteration in the b-verse:

> Þurgh sum lant goste-lyfe   of hym þat al redes (192)

Emendation of *al* to *lyfe* corrects it.[86]
Another three lines have just one alliterating lift in the a-verse:

> No3t bot fife hundred 3ere   þer aghtene wontyd (208)

The judge's figures cannot be right, but emendation of *fife* to *one* or *aght* does not improve them.

---

[84] See Putter et al. 2007, pp. 145–216.
[85] See the editions of *Destruction of Troy*, *Siege of Jerusalem*, *Wars of Alexander*. Putter et al. 2007, pp. 142–3 argue that this is true also of *Cleanness* and *Patience*.
[86] See the note on the difficulties of the line.

> Mony one was þe busmare   boden hom bitwene (214)

The first two words are perhaps an error for an adjective such as *Bitter*.

> Alle menyd my dethe   þe more and the lasse (247)

Alliteration is improved by emending *dethe* to *morte*, as in *Wars* 1402.
    Elision alliteration is uncommon in the poem. A clear example alliterating on /n/ is:

> I was an heire of anoye   in þe New Troie (211).

A less certain case is:

> Þagh I be vnworthi   al wepand he sayde (122)

Perhaps the spelling conceals 'Þow I' (ME *þo* plus a glide consonant, from ON **þóh*); cf. *þof* 320.

The B-Verse

The rhythmic structure of the first half-line appears to be more flexible than the second.[87] The general rule is that the second half-line must have two stressed syllables or lifts, and one, but only one, long dip: that is to say, an element of two or more unstressed syllables.[88] Using the standard notation, in which / is a stressed syllable, x an unstressed syllable, and (x) one or more additional unstressed syllables, the possible patterns are:

  1 ~xx(x)/x/x
  2 ~xx(x)//x
  3 ~x/xx(x)/x
  4 ~/xx(x)/x

Examples are:

  1 ~opon þe bothum lyggid (76)
  2 ~noȝt full long sythen (1)
  3 ~and Cristendome stablyd (2)
  4 ~blessyd and sacryd (3).

---

[87] For reflections on the A-verse see Inoue 2023.
[88] Duggan 1986.

These two basic patterns account for the great majority of b-verses in the poem. As in the verse of Chaucer and Gower, for the purpose of scansion word-final -e may be sounded when historically motivated, though scribal spellings are not a reliable guide.[89] Examples where -e is sounded are:

~halde my3t neuer (166) (OE infin. *haldan*)
~for bothe myn eghen (194) (ON *báðir*)
~and erthe bitwene (196) (OE *eorþe*)

A few apparent cases of verses with two long dips may be resolved by elision:

~by a visoun or elles (121) (elision of *by a*)
~3e are made for to lyuye (298) (elision of *3e are*)

In three cases the verse becomes regular by reading the reduced form *or* for conj. *oþir*:[90]

~oþir iuggid to pyne (188)
~oþir trowid euer shulde (255)
~oþir segge hyr to lathe (308)

But sometimes the full form is required:

~oþir moght-freten (86)

Dropping *þe* in '~and þe water þat þou sheddes' (329) corrects the metre with no detriment to sense; in '~of his grace summe brawnche' (276) *summe* is a monosyllable (OE *sum*), and there are other cases where spelling obscures the scansion.

A number of b-verses in the poem present the pattern with two short dips, ~x/x/x. Supplying a historically motivated final -e will regularise many of these: '~and last[e] so longe' (264; OE infin. *lastan*); '~þen sayd[e] þe bisshop' (273, cf. 282; OE *sǣde*). So too -e may be supplied in present participles ending in *-and* (from OE *-ende*, ON *-andi*) modifying a noun, as in '~with ryngand[e] noyce' (62; cf. '~with lauande teres' 314).[91]

---

[89] For details see Duggan 1986; Putter et al. 2007, pp. 73–101.
[90] See Duggan 1997, 233. The practice is frequent in *Pearl*.
[91] See Duggan 1988, 143.

Other verses of two short dips consist of a disyllabic adjective followed by a plural noun. It has been argued that these lines are authentic, a pattern inherited from a time when inflexions on adjectives of more than one syllable survived, but it is simpler to suppose that polysyllabic adjectives might retain their plural inflexion to satisfy the requirements of the metre.[92] Consequently, such verses with two short dips should be emended: '~in riall[e] wedes' (77), '~with eggit[e] toles' (40), '~with clustred[e] keies' (140). In '~with cumly bordures' (82) the adjective must have had a trisyllabic form, either *cumliche* or *cumely*;[93] in '~so kenely mony' (63) the adverb is trisyllabic, as in '~and kenely flowen' (*Cleanness* 945).[94] Polysyllabic adjectives from French retain -*e* as required, even if dropped by the scribe. For '~a **qu**ontyse strange' (74) compare *service*, a noun of similar shape in Chaucer: 'Ful weel she soong the service dyvyne' (*CT* I.122). However, emendation seems necessary for '~on sutile wise' (132) since the -*e* is not organic (OF *sotil*), most simply by reading *on a* (cf. *Gawain* 2048 '~and in a siker wyse') or *opon* (cf. *Gawain* 971); more adventurously by reading *solempne* for *sotile*, entirely appropriate in context and supported by *Cleanness* 1171 '~on solemne wyse'. Similarly, '~on gentil wise' (229) and '~in gentil lawe' (216) cannot be emended to *gentile* if derived from OF *gentil*, but the sense is 'gentile' from Lat. *gentilis* so that -*e* is historical; compare '~in gentyle wyse' (*Cleanness* 1432), and cf. 2 Macc. 4.10 'ad gentilem ritum', 'to the Gentile fashion'.[95] Two proper nouns should also be emended: '~in Hengyst[es] dawes' (7) and '~in Saxon[es] londes' (30) (cf. '~in Saxones tyme' 24).

The End of the Line

A majority of lines in alliterative verse end in a single unstressed syllable (a 'feminine' ending). Whether or not this is a requirement, a condition of metricality, is a subject of debate.[96] It is more than probable

---

[92] For the former view see Duggan 1988; for the latter, accepted here, see Putter et al. 2007, pp. 103–05.

[93] For the former interpretation see Putter et al. 2007, pp. 101–5; for the latter, adopted here, see the etymological discussion in *OED* s.v. *comely*.

[94] Putter et al. 2007, p. 110.

[95] *OED* has separate entries for *gentile* and *gentle*, confusingly conflated s.v. *gentil* in *MED*.

[96] Putter et al. 2007, pp. 19–71, and Yakovlev 2009 argue that it is a requirement; Duggan 2010 disagrees. Cornelius 2023, p. 261, states, perhaps incautiously, that 'the trochaic close is now a generally accepted feature of this meter'.

that the late scribe of *St Erkenwald* dropped inflectional endings in his copy, and where these can be easily restored it seems reasonable to do so. Thus, at the end of line 14 *newe* is adverbial (OE *nīwe*), so that lines ending *new* (6 and 37) can confidently be emended. Similarly, pa. t. *aght* (27) derives *-e* from OE *āhte*, as does the numeral *aght* (210) from OE *eahta*. In line 149 the line-end form *inne* gives support for emending *in* (326, 328; OE *inne, innan*).[97] *OED on* prep. notes the disyllabic form *onne* found especially in postposition, perhaps by analogy with *inne*, permitting the emendation of *þeron* to *þeronne* (79). Similarly, *þen* has been emended to *þenne* (OE *þanne*) in 118 and 212. As in Chaucerian verse, monosyllabic nouns such as *hert* (242, 257), that had a vowel or *-an* ending in OE (*heorte*), may retain *-e*, and following a preposition nouns may add *-e* (from the OE dative inflection) – for example, 'in his honde' (84), 'on benche' (250) and 'on fyrste' (207); therefore 'on fyrst' (144), 'to riȝt' (232) and 'out of ryȝt' (241) may be emended on the same basis.[98] Also 'þat wroghtyn ay riȝt' (301) may be emended to *riȝte* if it is understood as an adverb meaning 'rightly'. Twice the line ends in *þer* (94, 292); see *OED*'s etymology s.v. *there* adv. for ME *there*, perhaps from OE *þāra* rather than *þǣr*.[99] Line-terminal *þertill* (69, ON *til*) adds a non-etymological *-e* in *Cleanness* 1509 and *Gawain* 1110 (also 1369 in rhyme).[100] In verbs, the northern plural *has* (271) may be emended to the midland *haue* or *hauen* on the basis of pl. *haue* in 155; 3 sg. *shuld* (54) emended to *shulde* as in line-end *shulde* (255, OE *scolde*), infin. *tell* (114) to *telle* (OE *tellan*). Even *his* 174 has a disyllabic plural form *hise*, as in *Cleanness* 1216, on which see *MED his* pron.[101] To avoid a final long dip, there is syncope of *-en* in 'to herken hit' (134) and of the second *-o-* in *folowed* (351). In just three cases, pp. *bene* (26, OE *bēn*), *noght* (261), and *best* (272), no simple emendation suggests itself, and they are left to stand.[102]

---

[97] Cf. Putter et al. 2007, p. 29.
[98] See Putter et al. 2007, pp. 32–4.
[99] Putter et al. 2007, p. 30, and p. 74 n. 8.
[100] Cf. Putter et al. 2007, p. 30.
[101] Final *-e* has also been added to the nouns *laghe* (203, cf. 216, OE *lagu*), *feste* 303 (OF *feste*), adj. as pl. n. *trewe* (336, OE *trēowe*), pr. subj. *worthe* (340, OE *weorþe*), *longe* adv. (97), and *þen* emended to *þenne* (118, 212, OE *þanne*). It should be noted that, in line with their policy of expanding flourishes on some final consonants, Savage and Peterson have forms here treated as emendations; e.g. *shulde* 55, *þertille* 69, etc.
[102] Putter et al. 2007, pp. 58–9, focus on *St Erkenwald*, and discuss some of the 'remarkably few exceptions to the regular trochaic line ending'.

8. Structure and Style

Structure

The poem is a diptych of equal and contrasting panels, divided at exactly the mid point, recognised by the scribe by an enlarged capital at line 177. The first panel poses the question: who is this miraculously preserved body in the tomb unearthed by the builders? All is bustle and confusion, questioning and ignorance, 'quen matyd is monnes myȝt' (163) in the words of Erkenwald as he addresses the citizens at the end of the section. The second panel provides the answers, with the noisy activity replaced by the one-to-one conversation between the bishop and the body, with the crowd listening in silence. It ends with a dramatic baptism and the miraculous ringing of the bells throughout the city.[103]

The first act is subdivided into a prologue of thirty-two lines and two sections of seventy-two lines, the first of which gives an account of the discovery of the tomb, the second of Erkenwald's arrival in London, his night of prayer and his address to the people. The prologue (not marked as such by the scribe) offers a brisk introduction to the themes of the poem. In the opening two lines the place and the time are defined: these events happened in London not so very long ago, but, importantly, during the Christian era. Erkenwald is introduced as bishop, dismantling the heathendom of the Saxon invaders, completing the work of St Augustine the missionary in rededicating the pagan temples in Christ's name. Ancient London was called the New Troy, its temple occupied by a mighty devil. Time moves back and forth, the place goes through changes. Also introduced are the London people, *per*verted by the Saxons, *con*verted by Augustine. Their faith is weak and needs to be strengthened by the miracle that is to occur; they are excitable and troublesome, just as the Britons of London were treacherous and false and difficult to rule (231). The poem will end with the citizens united in orderly procession.

In the lines that follow the prologue, 'noȝt full long sythen' becomes *Now*, when Erkenwald *is* bishop of London, where he *teches* and *syttes*, so that the past has the relevance of the present. Deep in the foundations, the many workmen rebuilding St Paul's unearth a beautiful tomb with a clear but indecipherable inscription. There is noisy excitement as the news spreads and hundreds rush to see it, city officials, craftsmen,

---

[103] Aspects of structure and style are analysed by Petronella 1967, McAlindon 1970 and Burrow 1997.

apprentices and others, as if all the world had gathered. The mayor and sexton order the lid to be opened and there is revealed a body richly dressed and with crown and sceptre, as fresh as if he had fallen asleep the day before. This causes wild excitement and confusion: who could this possibly be?

In the last part of this first act Erkenwald, who is visiting an abbey in Essex, is summoned back to quell the 'troubull in þe pepul' (109). To the surprise of the welcoming committee, instead of listening to the babble of voices and investigating the 'toumbe wonder' (57), he shuts himself in his palace for the night, praying that the Holy Spirit will give him an answer to confirm the fragile faith of the populace. In the morning, robed in his episcopal vestments, he sings high mass before a congregation drawn from the whole realm. Only then does he move to the tomb, guided by the dean, who explains that, despite all their research, they cannot discover anything about the identity of the body. In his reply that concludes the first half of the poem, Erkenwald explains that mankind's feeble powers are as nothing in respect of almighty God, whose powers the bishop will demonstrate in order to buttress the people's faith.

Act two opens as Erkenwald at last 'turnes to the toumbe' to question the body. This half of the poem may be divided into four sections of forty-four lines, each with a brief question from the bishop and a longer response from the body. Firstly Erkenwald asks the body in the name of Christ to answer four questions: who he was, how long he has lain there, what his religion was and whether his soul is in heaven or hell (177–88); the body prepares to speak (189–92), answering that he was a judge in ancient pagan times under the British king Belin (193–216); the people listen in silence (217–20). The judge's speech is exactly twice as long as Erkenwald's, and each is followed by a comment of four lines.

In the second movement the bishop asks why, as a judge, he wears a crown and holds a sceptre (221–4); the judge replies at length that these were assigned to him because he was the most just of all justices (225–56); Erkenwald supposes that the body may have been embalmed, but questions how the clothing could have survived undamaged (257–64).

In the third movement the judge explains that God who loves justice above all has preserved him (265–72). Erkenwald, speaking at the same length, returns to the question of the judge's soul, and of God's rich reward, which is clearly merited (273–80). Heartbreakingly, the judge replies that as a pagan he had no knowledge of God's covenant, so he was not redeemed when Christ visited limbo to release the souls of his followers. Instead he remains in that dark place while those descendants of Adam whose sins have been washed away by baptism are redeemed. All his good works count for nothing, exiled as he is from the heavenly banquet (282–308).

The final section prepares for the accidental baptism by describing the general weeping of the observers, especially the bishop, unable to speak for tears (309–14). Then, looking at the body, Erkenwald says 'If only God would grant that you could hold on to life until I fetch water and baptise you in the name of the Father and the Son and the Holy Spirit' (315–20). With those words Erkenwald's tear splashes onto the judge's face. The judge praises God and the Virgin, as well as the bishop who has baptised him with his tear, so that now his soul is seated at the banquet in heaven (321–40). The body is suddenly reduced to powder, for it is worthless in the context of everlasting life. With a mixture of grief and joy the people praise God, and the bells of the town ring out (341–52).

This tight and balanced structure maintains the mystery and suspense of the narrative throughout, as expectations are repeatedly defeated. The tomb with its mysterious decoration and inscription is uncovered, but the excited onlookers must wait until the arrival of the mayor before – with effort and skill – the tomb may be opened. To their amazement, the body inside is as fresh as if it were asleep, and is richly dressed as a lawyer, yet puzzlingly with regal crown and sceptre. There is agitation, as no-one can explain it or identify the body. Crucially, Erkenwald is away, and in his absence there is nobody with spiritual authority to turn to. Everyone looks to the bishop to become master of the situation on his return. Surely he will immediately resolve the matter? But he ignores the tomb and spends the night praying for understanding of 'þe mysterie of þis meruaile' (125) before receiving 'an ansuare of the Holy Goste' (127), not revealed to us. Even now Erkenwald delays the action by celebrating high mass. Finally he turns to the body and expresses his perplexity, not at the preservation of the body, which could be embalmed, but the freshness of the clothing, which should surely have rotted away. On learning that the judge had been preserved for his exemplary pursuit of justice, Erkenwald naturally assumes that his soul is enjoying the bliss of heaven, but learns that, since the judge was an unbaptised pagan, his soul is in the darkness of limbo. The accidental baptism that follows is the final surprise, as the body with all its solidity and rich accoutrements dissolves into powder.

The smallest structural unit is the four-line 'sentence' as a way of shaping and pacing the narrative. *Erkenwald* shares this practice with *Siege*, *Wars*, *Patience* and *Cleanness*. Yet this is a flexible arrangement, and every now and then the poet will have a longer or shorter 'sentence' before resuming the four-line scheme. In *Cleanness* and *Siege* the syntax may sometimes overstep the unit (e.g. *Cleanness* 1540–5, 1586–92, *Siege* 576–81); similarly in *Erkenwald* two units of five lines (117–121 and 150–4) are resolved by a two-line unit (167–8) so that the first act ends on a multiple of four (176). Editors sometimes set out these poems in four-line 'stanzas', as did Gollancz and Savage, but this over-emphasises the divisions, which are better defined by punctuation.

Stylistic Features

The style of alliterative poetry is characteristically expansive and leisurely, with detailed descriptions and use of 'variation', of which a classic example is the introduction of Youth in *The Parlement of the Thre Ages*:

> The first was a ferse freke, fayrere than thies othire,
> A bolde beryn one a blonke bownne for to ryde,
> A hathelle on ane heghe horse with hauke appon hande.
> (109–11)

[The first was a fierce warrior, handsomer than the others, a bold fellow on a steed, equipped to ride, a man on a high horse with hawk on hand.]

This static portrait features synonymy and variation, parallelism of syntax and the slow accumulation of information. Youth is successively 'a ferse freke', 'a bolde beryn' and 'a hathelle'; he is 'one a blonke' and 'on ane heghe horse'; equipped to ride, he holds a hawk. Though there are traces of this leisurely and formulaic style in *Erkenwald*, as in the description of the body discovered in the tomb (75–92), the fact that so much happens in 352 lines indicates that economy of style is more characteristic of the poem. Successive lines are 'information rich' and show more forward movement:

> Laddes laften hor werke and lepen þiderwardes,
> Ronnen radly in route with ryngande noyce;
> Þer comen þider of all kynnes so kenely mony
> Þat as all þe worlde were þider walon within a honde-quile.
> (61–4)

They leave, they leap, they run, they come, but around this variation we are constantly given more information. Paratactic constructions are characteristic of scenes of action, where the alliteration throws emphasis on the content-words:

> Wyȝt werkemen with þat wenten þertille,
> Putten prises þerto, pinchid one-vnder,
> Kaghten by þe corners with crowes of yrne,
> And were þe lydde neuer so large þai laide hit by sone. (69–72)

Following the subject *werkemen*, the verbs *wenten*, *putten* and *kaghten* describe step by step the procedure of raising the tomb. These workmen are constructing the so-called 'New Werke' (38), and both words run through the opening lines, for it is a new beginning, a time when the pagan temple is to be consecrated anew (6), Londoners to be converted anew (14) in what was 'þe New Troie' (25), and the temple to be 'buggyd efte new' (37).

With the basic structure consisting of two balanced and contrasting halves, balance and contrasts run through the poem, heightening the effect of oppositional pairs: light/dark, joy/sorrow, open/closed.[104] The play between light and dark is particularly effective, occurring at key moments. To everyone's surprise and sadness the judge's soul is 'dwynande in þe derke deth' (294) rather than in heaven, an expression repeated as 'dymly in þat derke dethe' (306); but with the baptism from 'þe bryȝt bourne of þin eghen' (330) 'liȝtly lasshit þer a leme' (334) that spirited his soul to heaven. Noises sweet and jarring are heard throughout the poem:[105] in the first half the 'ryngande noyce' (62) of the excited lads, the 'cry aboute a cors' that 'crakit' (110), that Erkenwald must quell; in the second half the 'day-belle' that signifies the end of 'þe derke nyȝt' (117), the lovely voices of the choir singing high mass 'with ful quaynt notes' (133), the 'drery dreme' (191) of the body as it speaks, the silence of the people listening to the judge:

> þer sprange in þe pepull
> In al þis worlde no worde ne wakenyd no noice,
> Bot al as stille as þe ston stoden and listonde. (217–19)

Finally, in the last line, the joyful sound of all the bells in the town resounds (352).

---

[104] Explored by Petronella 1967, 535–6.
[105] See Bugbee 2008.

In a poem with such varied vocabulary, repetition stands out as stylistically significant. Most prominent is the repetition of *riȝt*, 'what is right, justice, just action', and as the adverb 'justly'. It is the judge's highest boast that he never deviated 'fro þe riȝt', never 'glent out of ryȝte' (235, 241). Though he had no knowledge of the Supreme Judge, his exemplary justice represents God's as far as was possible for a pagan judge. Crowned 'kynge of kene justices' (254), his justice echoed that of

> Þe riche kyng of reson, þat riȝt euer alowes,
> And loues al þe lawes lely þat longen to trouthe;
> And moste he menskes men for mynnyng of riȝtes
> Þen for al þe meritorie medes þat men on molde vsen;
> And if renkes for riȝt þus me arayed has,
> He has lant me to last þat loues ryȝt best. (267–72)

In this artful repetition with variation, the word *riȝt* is pervasive, occupying a different position in the line each time, as God's *riȝt*, as the judge's *riȝt* in recognition of which his body has remained intact.[106] In his reply, Erkenwald is perhaps recalling the biblical 'There is laid up for me a crown of justice [*corona iustitiae*] which the Lord the just judge will render to me in that day' (2 Timothy 4.8). It seems obvious that this exemplary figure should have received his crown of justice:

> He þat rewardes vche a renke as he has riȝt seruyd
> Myȝt euel forgo the to gyfe of his grace summe brawnche.
> (275–6)

Then follows the shocking news that the judge has *not* been saved. We must sympathise with the judge's plaintive lament, 'Quat wan we with oure wele-dede þat wroghtyn ay riȝte' (301). If his supreme justice, the virtue that God himself represents, cannot save him, what can?

Case Study (1): Bishop Erkenwald's Speech

Erkenwald's magnificent speech comes at the end of the first act, at a pivotal point, the transition from busy human activity to the solemn demonstration of God's power. It is skilfully crafted. Having spent the night in prayer, Erkenwald is granted an answer from the Holy Spirit, and the next morning he offers a votive mass in honour of the Holy

---

[106] Lines discussed by Putter et al. 2007, pp. 161–2.

Spirit. In his address to the people, his references to God are specifically to the third person of the Trinity, as expressed by his allusion to two biblical epithets for the Holy Spirit, 'Finger of God' and 'Comforter' (a translation of 'Paraclete').[107]

The dean, pointing 'wyt fynger' to the tomb, expresses his bewilderment at the significance of the body. Erkenwald replies that what is beyond human comprehension is as nothing to God, who can unlock the mystery with a finger, in derisive contrast to the dean's useless finger. The reference is to the verse in Luke 11.20, 'I, by the finger of God [in digito dei], cast out devils', which is understood as referring to the power of the Holy Spirit. So, in the famous hymn 'Veni Creator Spiritus', the Holy Spirit is 'digitus paternae dexterae', translated by William Herebert as 'vinger of godes honde'.[108] Of course men are perplexed, 'but the Paraclete, the Holy Ghost, whom the Father will send in my name, he will teach you all things' (John 14.26), a verse translated by the Wycliffite Bible as 'but thilke Hooli Ghost, the coumfortour, whom the fadir schal sende in my name, he schal teche 3ou alle thingis'. Coincidentally, another poem from Harley 2250 explains 'Paraclitus is as mych to say / As comfortour' (*Stanzaic Life of Christ* 10753–4), so called because the Holy Spirit sends succour to the sorrowful. So, when the bishop speaks of 'þe comforth of þe Creatore', he means in general God's beneficence and in particular the Holy Spirit himself, an interpretation strengthened by the parallel from Langland, who says the Holy Ghost is 'confortour of creatures' (*Piers Plowman* B.16.198).

As bishop, Erkenwald will reveal God's powers to confirm the faith of his people. His speech is structured as a central couplet defining his argument, sandwiched between four 'sentences' of four lines, the first two summing up the event of the first half of the poem, the last two pointing forward to the doctrine of the second half.

The first 'sentence' sets up the contrast between *men* and *þe Prince*, and continues the idea of locking and unlocking in the first half of the poem: the literal unlocking of the lid of the sarcophagus (*vnlouke* 67), the body enclosed (*loken* 147) in the coffin, and now in a figurative sense of *vnlouke*, the release of God's *my3tes*. The second 'sentence' immediately picks up the word *my3te*, contrasting *monnes* powers with God's and pairing it with *mynde*, human intellect so easily overcome, echoing the dean's acknowledgement of the limitations of the *mynde* (151 and 154). The verb *louse* continues the image of releasing power, now figured as

---

[107] See Borroff 2006b, 140.
[108] Herebert, *Works*, ed. Reimer 1987, 8.5.

God's finger, which then becomes a metonymy that is replaced by all the hands under heaven, the powers of all humankind that, with a direct contrast to *louse*, could never *halde* the powers that God had released.

The central couplet begins with *þereas*, 'in a situation in which', stating the problem and then providing the solution. The two lines alliterate on /k/ and play upon the traditional antithetical chime of *creatures/creatore*, as for example in Romans 1.25 condemning those who worshipped and served creatures (*creaturae*) rather than the Creator (*Creatori*), and in *Piers Plowman* B.16.224, 'Creator wex creature'. Feeble human power, 'creatures crafte', synonymous with 'monnes my3te', swerves away from *counsell*, 'understanding', and so God's *comforth* must provide the remedy. Both *counsell* and *comforth* are to be picked up in the lines that follow.

In the final lines Erkenwald concludes that in the face of human impotence we must cease speculation and instead must call upon God for his *counsell* and *comforth*, for he is *my3ty*. In his conclusion, to underline the importance of *faith*, the bishop continues with the synonym *bileue*, followed by the associated verb *leue* in two successive lines. His purpose as bishop is to strengthen the faith of his wayward people with a sign granted by the Holy Spirit, in line with John 20.30, 'that you may believe that Jesus is the Christ, the Son of God'.

Case Study (2): The Baptism

The unusual baptism is both the climax of the story and the resolution of the issues raised, so that previous actions and descriptions are concluded, often as contrasts. With subtle use of progressive variation, 'þis dede body' (309), 'þe liche' (314) and the 'faire cors' (317) become 'þe freke' (323), the man who speaks his final words. In a contrary movement, the face that was as fresh and ruddy 'as þe rose' (91) now in a double simile becomes 'blakke as þe moldes' and 'roten as þe rottok' (343–4), mere flesh and vanity subject to earthly decay.

The focus of these last lines is upon the unorthodox source of water for the baptism. All the people 'weped for woo' (310) as they listened to the judge's sad story, not least the bishop, 'so spakly he 3oskyd' (312). He utters the baptismal formula 'with lauande teres' (314), with flowing tears, but also with spiritually cleansing tears.[109] Then 'þe wete of his eghen and teres' fall, and one lands on the judge's face (321). Now 'þe

---

[109] *MED laven* 1(a) cites Idley's *Instructions*: 'Ther bodies with baptisme than to be laved'.

water' becomes, in the judge's words, 'þe bry3t bourne of þin eghen' (330), the river metaphor capturing the significance of the tear, uniting it with Christ's own baptism in the river Jordan. This, continues the judge, is 'þe water þat wesche vs of payne' (333), with the metaphor reviving the suggestion of the 'lauande teres'.

The climax of the poem is one of emotional contrasts: the *woo* of the observers is countered by the *murthe* of the judge's soul; the movement is 'fro bale ... to blis' (340), and finally 'meche mournyng and myrthe was mellyd togeder' (350). The 'derke deth' (294 and 306) of limbo is resolved by the flash of light that signals the judge's salvation (334), while the hunger in *helle-hole* is satisfied by the heavenly banquet that greets the soul. We are conscious throughout of the audience whose faith is strengthened by what they see and hear, the Londoners no longer an unruly crowd but a solemn procession passing away from the scene. And finally the bells of the town miraculously ring out, resolving the variety of sounds in the poem: the 'ryngande noyce' (62), the 'cry aboute a cors' (110), and the *day-belle* (118) presaging Erkenwald's intervention.

9. Treatment of the Text

Capitalisation and word-division have been brought into line with modern practice, and punctuation and paragraphing have been added. The half-lines have been separated by a double space. An acute accent has been added to the final *e* in *sayntuaré*, *debonerté*, *cité* and *honesté* from OF. The scribe uses the standard abbreviations and suspensions, which have been expanded without notice in line with the scribe's full forms, except that w^t is expanded to *with* despite the scribal form *wyt* in 165 and 341. Flourishes on final consonants have been ignored, except for the loop on *r* which indicates *re* (contrast *here* 13 with loop and *hor* 17 without). All emendations are recorded in the variants listed at the foot of the page. These include emendations made to correct the metre, as explained in section 7 above.

Bibliography

Primary Sources

Annales monastici, ed. H. R. Luard (Rolls Series, London, 1864)

Aquinas, *Commentary on the Sentences* and *Summa Theologiae*, aquinasinstitute.org/aquinas-opera-omnia

Aquinas, *Quaestiones Disputatae, de Veritate*, Isidore.co/aquinas

Augustine, *Contra Julianum*, PL 44. 751

Bede's Ecclesiastical History, ed. and transl. Bertram Colgrave and R. A. B. Mynors (Oxford, 1969)

A Bird in Bishopswood, ed. Ruth Kennedy, in *Medieval Literature and Antiquities*, ed. Myra Stokes and T. L. Burton (Cambridge, 1987), pp. 71–87

Bradshaw, Henry, *The Life of St Werburge of Chester*, ed. C. Horstmann, EETS OS 88 (1887)

Brown 1957: Carleton Brown, ed., *Religious Lyrics of the XIVth Century*, 2nd edn (Oxford)

Charter of the Abbey of the Holy Ghost, ed. C. Horstman, *Yorkshire Writers* 1 (London, 1985), pp. 337–62

Chaucer, Geoffrey, *The Riverside Chaucer*, ed. Larry D. Benson (Boston, 1987)

The Chester Mystery Cycle, ed. R. M. Lumiansky and David Mills, EETS SS 3 and SS 9 (1974, 1986)

Cleanness, ed. J. J. Anderson (Manchester, 1977)

Compendium Theologicae veritatis (Speyer, 1473)

Dante: The Divine Comedy, ed. and transl. John D. Sinclair, 3 vols (London, 1948)

Death and Liffe, ed. Joseph M. Donatelli (Cambridge, MA, 1989)

The Destruction of Troy, ed. Hiroyuki Matsumoto (3rd edn, Okayama-shi, 2011)

The Digby Poems, ed. Helen Barr (Exeter, 2009)

The Earliest Life of Gregory the Great, ed. and transl. Bertram Colgrave (Lawrence, KS, 1968)

Fiore di filosofi e di molti savi, ed. Antonio Cappelli (Bologna, 1865)

Fortescue: John Fortescue, *De Laudibus Legum Anglie*, ed. and transl. S. B. Chrimes (Cambridge, 1942)

Geoffrey of Monmouth: The History of the Kings of Britain, transl. Lewis Thorpe (Harmondsworth, 1966)

Gilte Legende, ed. Richard Hamer, vol. 1, EETS OS 327 (2006)

Guido da Pisa, dantelab.dartmouth.edu/reader

Herebert, William: *The Works of William Herebert*, ed. Stephen R. Reimer (Toronto, 1987)

Higden, Ranulf: *Polychronicon Ranulphi Higden*, ed. C. Babington and J. R. Lumby, Rolls Series (1865–86)

A History of the Chantries Within the County Palatine of Lancaster, ed. Francis Robert Raines, Chetham Society OS 59 (Manchester, 1862)

Innocent III, *De miseria conditionis humane*, ed. Robert E. Lewis (Athens, GA, 1978)

Isidore: *Isidori Hispalensis Episcopi Etymologiarvm sive Originvm*, ed. W. M. Lindsay (Oxford, 1911)

Jacobus de Voragine: *Jacobi a Voragine: Legenda Aurea*, ed. T. Graesse (Dresden, 1846)

Laȝamon, *Brut*, ed. G. L. Brook and R. F. Leslie, EETS OS 250 and 277 (1963, 1968)

Lancashire and Cheshire Wills and Inventories, from the Ecclesiastical Court, Chester, 1 and 2, ed. George John Piccope, Chetham Society OS 33, 51 (Manchester, 1857, 1860)

The Lay Folks' Catechism, ed. T. F. Simmons and H. E. Nolloth, EETS OS 118 (1901)

Livy: *Ab urbe condita*, book 5, ed. R. I. Ross (London, 1996)

Matthew Paris, *Chronica Majora*, transl. J. A. Giles, *Matthew Paris's English History*, 3 vols (London, 1852–4)

— *Gesta Abbatum Monasterii Sancti Albani*, ed. Henry Thomas Riley, 3 vols (London, 1867–9)

— *The Life of St Alban*, transl. Jocelyn Wogan Browne and Thelma S. Fenster (New York, 2010)

Mannyng: *Robert Mannyng of Brunne, The Chronicle*, ed. Idelle Sullens (Binghamton, 1996)

— *Robert of Brunne's Handlyng Synne*, ed. Frederick J. Furnivall, EETS OS 119, 123 (1901, 1903)

Memoriale Credencium, ed. J. H. L. Kengen (Nijmegen, 1979)

Mirk: *John Mirk's Festial*, ed. Susan Powell, 2 vols, EETS OS 334, 335 (2009, 2011)

The Parlement of the Thre Ages, in *Alliterative Poetry of the Later Middle Ages*, ed. Thorlac Turville-Petre (London, 1989), pp. 67–100

Patience, ed. J. J. Anderson (Manchester, 1969)

Pearl, ed. Thorlac Turville-Petre (Liverpool, 2021)
Piers Plowman, the A-Version, ed. George Kane (London, 1960); *William Langland, Piers Plowman: The B-Version Archetype*, ed. J. A. Burrow and Thorlac Turville-Petre (Raleigh, NC, 2018); *Piers Plowman by William Langland: An Edition of the C-Text*, ed. Derek Pearsall (London, 1978)
The Prick of Conscience, ed. Ralph Hanna and Sarah Wood, EETS OS 342 (2013)
Richard the Redeless, in *Mum and the Sothsegger*, ed. Mabel Day and Robert Steele EETS OS 199 (1936)
Robbins 1952: Rossell Hope Robbins, ed., *Secular Lyrics of the XIV and XV Centuries* (Oxford)
Rolevinck, Werner, *De laude antiquae Saxonicae nunc Westphaliae dictae*, ed. Hermann Bücher (Münster, 1953)
St Editha, ed. Carl Horstmann (Heilbronn, 1883)
St Erkenwald, ed. Sir Israel Gollancz (London, 1922)
— ed. H. L. Savage (New Haven, CT, 1926)
— ed. Ruth Morse (Cambridge, 1975)
— ed. Clifford Peterson (Philadelphia, 1977)
— ed. Thorlac Turville-Petre, *Alliterative Poetry of the Later Middle Ages* (London, 1989), pp. 101–19
— ed. Thorlac Turville-Petre and J. A. Burrow, *A Book of Middle English* (4th edn, Chichester, 2021), pp. 233–46
Saint Etheldreda, ed. Carl Horstmann, *Altenglische Legenden, Neue Folge* (Heilbronn, 1881), pp. 282–307
Sarum Missal, ed. J. Wickham Legg (Oxford, 1916)
S. Bonaventurae opera omnia, ed. A. C. Peltier (Paris, 1864–71)
The Siege of Jerusalem, ed. Ralph Hanna and David Lawton, EETS OS 320 (2003)
Sir Gawain and the Green Knight, ed. J. R. R. Tolkien and E. V. Gordon, rev. Norman Davis (2nd edn, Oxford, 1967)
— ed. Sir Israel Gollancz, EETS OS 210 (1940)
The South English Legendary, ed. Charlotte d'Evelyn and Anna J. Mill, 3 vols, EETS OS 235–6, 241 (1957, 1959)
Speculum Christiani, ed. Gustaf Holmstedt, EETS OS 182 (1933)
A Stanzaic Life of Christ, ed. Frances A. Foster, EETS OS 166 (1926)
Victoria County History of Lancaster, ed. William Farrer and J. Brownbill, vol. 4 (London, 1911)
Wace's Roman de Brut, A History of the British, ed. Judith Weiss (2nd edn, Exeter, 2002)
Walsingham, Thomas, *Historia Anglicana*, ed. H. T. Riley (London, 1863–4)
The Wars of Alexander, ed. Hoyt N. Duggan and Thorlac Turville-Petre, EETS SS 10 (1989)

Wycliffite Bible, ed. Forshall and F. Madden, *The Holy Bible ... in the Earliest English Versions*, 4 vols (Oxford, 1850)
Wynnere and Wastoure, in *Alliterative Poetry of the Later Middle Ages*, ed. Thorlac Turville-Petre (London, 1989), pp. 38-66

Secondary Sources

Adams 1988: Robert Adams, 'Langland's Theology', in *A Companion to Piers Plowman*, ed. John A. Alford (Berkeley), pp. 87-114
Alford 1988a: John A. Alford, *Piers Plowman: A Glossary of Legal Diction* (Cambridge)
— 1988b: 'The Idea of Reason in *Piers Plowman*', in *Medieval English Studies Presented to George Kane*, ed. Donald Kennedy et al. (Cambridge), pp. 199-215
Baker 2013: John Baker, 'English Judges' Robes 1350-2008', in *Collected Papers in English Legal History* (Cambridge), 2, ch. 45
Barnes and Page 2006: Michael P. Barnes and R. I. Page, *The Scandinavian Runic Inscriptions of Britain* (Uppsala)
Barron 2003: Caroline Barron, 'London and St Paul's Cathedral', in *The Medieval English Cathedral*, ed. Janet Backhouse (Donington), pp. 126-49
Barry 1915: Phillips Barry, 'Bells Ringing Without Hands', *Modern Language Notes* 30, 28-9
Benson 1965: L. D. Benson, 'The Authorship of *St Erkenwald*', *JEGP* 64, 393-405
Borroff 1962: Marie Borroff, *Sir Gawain and the Green Knight: A Stylistic and Metrical Study* (New Haven, CT)
— 2006a: 'Narrative Artistry in *St Erkenwald* and the *Gawain*-Group', *Studies in the Age of Chaucer* 28, 41-76
— 2006b: '*St Erkenwald*: Narrative and Narrative Artistry', in *Mindful Spirit in Late Medieval Literature*, ed. Bonnie Wheeler (New York), pp. 135-48
Brand 2001: Paul Brand, 'Ethical Standards for Royal Justices in England, c. 1175-1307', *Roundtable: The University of Chicago Law School* 8, 239-79
Breeze 2008: Andrew Breeze, 'Art "Direction" in *St Erkenwald*', *N&Q* 55, 273-4
— 2009: '*Skelt* "Hasten" in *Cleanness* and *St Erkenwald*', *Leeds Studies in English* n.s. 40, 147-8
Bugbee 2008: John Bugbee, 'Sight and Sound in *St Erkenwald*: On Theodicy and the Senses', *MÆ* 77, 202-21
Burnley 1983: David Burnley, *A Guide to Chaucer's Language* (London)
Burrow 1971: J. A. Burrow, *Ricardian Poetry* (London)
— 1993: '*Saint Erkenwald* Line 1: "At London in Englond"', *N&Q* 40, 22-3

— 1997: 'Redundancy in Alliterative Verse: *St Erkenwald*', in *Individuality and Achievement in Middle English Poetry*, ed. O. S. Pickering (Cambridge), pp. 119–28

— 2004: '*St Erkenwald* lines 231–244', *N&Q* 51, 347–8

Cable 1991: Thomas Cable, *The English Alliterative Tradition* (Philadelphia)

Campbell 2018: Ethan Campbell, *The Gawain-Poet and the Fourteenth-Century English Anticlerical Tradition* (Kalamazoo, MI)

Clark 1951: John W. Clark, 'On Certain "Alliterative" and "Poetic" Words in the Poems Attributed to "The Gawain Poet"', *Modern Language Quarterly* 12, 387–98

Clayton 1990: Dorothy J. Clayton, *The Administration of the County Palatine of Chester, 1442–1485*, Chetham Soc., 3rd ser., 35 (Manchester)

Cornelius 2023: Ian Cornelius, 'It's Complicated: Some Irregular Line-Ending Morphosyllabic Sequences in *Piers Plowman* B', *ChR* 58, 259–82

Dance 2019: Richard Dance, *Words Derived from Old Norse in Sir Gawain and the Green Knight: An Etymological Survey* (Chichester)

Duffy 2018: Eamon Duffy, '*St Erkenwald*', in *Royal Books and Holy Bones* (London), pp. 165–86

Duggan 1986: Hoyt N. Duggan, 'The Shape of the B-Verse in Middle English Alliterative Poetry', *Speculum* 61, 564–92

— 1988: 'Final -*e* and the Rhythmic Structure of the B-Verse in Middle English Alliterative Poetry', *MP* 86, 119–45

— 1997: 'Metre, Stanza, Vocabulary, Dialect', in *A Companion to the Gawain Poet*, ed. Derek Brewer and Jonathan Gibson (Cambridge), pp. 221–42

— 2010: 'The End of the Line', in *Medieval Alliterative Poetry*, ed. John A. Burrow and Hoyt N. Duggan (Dublin), pp. 67–79

Gibson 2013: Marion Gibson, *Imagining the Pagan Past* (Abingdon)

Gillespie 1980: Vincent Gillespie, '*Doctrina* and *Predicacio*: The Design and Function of Some Pastoral Manuals', *Leeds Studies in English* 11, 36–50

— 2008: 'Chapter and Worse: An Episode in the Regional Transmission of the *Speculum Christiani*', in *Regional Manuscripts, 1200–1700*, ed. A. S. G. Edwards (London: British Library, 2008), pp. 86–110

Görlach 1974: Manfred Görlach, *The Textual Tradition of the South English Legendary* (Leeds)

Grady 1992: Frank Grady, '*Piers Plowman*, *St Erkenwald* and the Rule of Exeptional Salvations', *Yearbook of Langland Studies* 6, 61–86

— 2005: *Representing Righteous Heathens in Late Medieval England* (New York)

Harbus 2002: Antonia Harbus, *Helena of Britain in Medieval Legend* (Cambridge)

Harrod 1900: H. D. Harrod, 'A Defence of the Liberties of Chester, 1450', *Archaeologia* 57, 71–86

Holland 1633: Henry Holland, *Ecclesia Sancti Pauli illustrata* (London)

Horobin 2017: Simon Horobin, 'Langland's Dialect Reconsidered', in *Pursuing Middle English Manuscripts and Their Texts*, ed. Simon Horobin and Aditi Nafde (Turnhout), pp. 63–76

Iannucci 2005: Amilcare A. Iannucci, 'Dante's Limbo: At the Margins of Orthodoxy', in *Dante and the Unorthodox*, ed. James Miller (Waterloo, Ontario, Canada), pp. 63–82

Inoue 2032: Noriko Inoue, 'The "Extra Long" Dip in the Poems of the *Gawain* Poet', ChR 58, 232–58

Jones 2017: Mike Rodman Jones, 'Articulating the Psalms in Middle English Alliterative Poetry', in *The Psalms and Middle English Literature*, ed. Tamara Atkin and Francis Lenegan (Cambridge), pp. 233–52

Kamowski 1995: William Kamowski, '*St Erkenwald* and the Inadvertent Baptism: An Orthodox Response to Heterodox Ecclesiology', *Religion and Literature* 27 no. 3, 5–27

Ker 1964: N. R. Ker, *Medieval Libraries of Great Britain*, 2nd edn (London)
— 1969: *Medieval Manuscripts in British Libraries*, vol. 1 (Oxford)

Kerby-Fulton 2021: Kathryn Kerby-Fulton, *The Clerical Proletariat and the Resurgence of Medieval English Poetry* (Philadelphia, PA)

Kreuzer 1938: James R. Kreuzer, 'Some Earlier Examples of the Rhetorical Device in *Ralph Roister Doister* (III. iv. 33ff.)', *Review of English Studies* 14, 321–3

Luttrell 1958: C. A. Luttrell, 'Three North-West Midland Manuscripts', *Neophilologus* 42, 38–50

McAlindon 1970: T. McAlindon, 'Hagiography into Art', *Studies in Philology* 67, 472–94

McCulloch 1981: Florence McCulloch, 'Saints Alban and Amphibalus in the Works of Matthew Paris: Dublin, Trinity College MS 177', *Speculum* 56, 761–85

Marenbon 2015a: John Marenbon, 'Virtuous Pagans, Hopeless Desire and Unjust Justice', in *Vertical Readings in Dante's Comedy*, ed. George Corbett and Heather Webb (Cambridge), vol. 1, pp. 77–96
— 2015b: *Pagans and Philosophers: The Problem of Paganism from Augustine to Leibniz* (Princeton, NJ)

Mustanoja 1960: Tauno F. Mustanoja, *A Middle English Syntax* (Helsinki)

Newhauser and Bolton 2012: Richard Newhauser and William E. Bolton, 'A Hybrid Life of John the Baptist: The Middle English Text of MS Harley 2250', *Anglia*, 130, 218–39

Oakden 1930, 1935: J. P. Oakden, *Alliterative Poetry in Middle English*, 2 vols (Manchester)

O'Loughlin and Conrad-O'Briain 1993: T. O'Loughlin and H. Conrad-O'Briain, 'The "Baptism of Tears" in Early Anglo-Saxon Sources', *Anglo-Saxon England* 22, 65–83

Otter 1994: Monika Otter, '"Newe Werke": *St Erkenwald*, St Albans, and the Medieval Sense of the Past', *Journal of Medieval and Renaissance Studies* 24, 387–414
— 1996: *Inventiones: Fiction and Referentiality in Twelfth-Century English Historical Writing* (Chapel Hill, NC)
Padoan 1969: Giorgio Padoan, 'Il Limbo Dantesco', *Lettere Italiane* 21, 369–88
Pearsall 1977: Derek Pearsall, *Old English and Middle English Poetry* (London)
Petronella 1967: Vincent F. Petronella, 'Style as the Vehicle for Meaning', *JEGP* 66, 532–40
Putter 1995: Ad Putter, *Sir Gawain and the Green Knight and French Arthurian Romance* (Oxford)
— 2006: 'The Ways and Words of the Hunt', *ChR* 40, 354–85
Putter and Stokes 2007: Ad Putter and Myra Stokes, 'The *Linguistic Atlas* and the Dialect of the *Gawain* Poems', *JEGP* 106, 468–91
Putter et al. 2007: Ad Putter, Judith Jefferson and Myra Stokes, *Studies in the Metre of Alliterative Verse* (Oxford)
Quinn 1984a: W. A. Quinn, 'The Psychology of *St Erkenwald*', *MÆ* 53, 180–93
— 1984b: 'A Liturgical Detail and an Alternative Reading of *St Erkenwald* Line 319', *Review of English Studies*, 335–41
Saul 2009: Nigel Saul, *English Church Monuments in the Middle Ages* (Oxford)
Scattergood 2017: John Scattergood, '"St Erkenwald" and Its Literary Relations', in *Saints and Cults in Medieval England*, ed. Susan Powell (Donington), pp. 339–62
Schofield 2011: John Schofield, *St Paul's Cathedral: Archaeology and History* (Oxford)
Shelby 1964: L. R. Shelby, 'The Role of the Master Mason in Mediaeval English Building', *Speculum* 39, 387–403
Sisk 2007: Jennifer L. Sisk, 'The Uneasy Orthodoxy of *St Erkenwald*', *English Literary History* 74, 89–115
Spearing 1970: A. C. Spearing, *The Gawain-Poet* (Cambridge)
Stow 1908: John Stow, *A Survey of London (1603)*, edited C. L. Kingsford (Oxford)
Tatlock 1914: John S. P. Tatlock, 'Notes on Chaucer', *Modern Language Notes* 29, 97–101
Turner 2006: Marion Turner, *Chaucerian Conflict* (Oxford)
Turville-Petre 1977: Thorlac Turville-Petre, *The Alliterative Revival* (Cambridge)
— 2005: '*St Erkenwald* and the Crafty Chronicles', in *Studies in Late Medieval and Early Renaissance Texts*, ed. Anne Marie D'Arcy and Alan J. Fletcher (Dublin), pp. 362–74

— 2008: 'St Erkenwald and the Judicial Oath', N&Q 55, 19–21
— 2018: *Description and Narrative in Middle English Alliterative Poetry* (Liverpool)
— 2023a: 'St Erkenwald and the Judge in Limbo', ChR 58, 348–60
— 2023b: 'BL MS Harley 2250: A Fifteenth-Century Cheshire Miscellany', *Nottingham Medieval Studies* 67, 229–46
Wanley 1759: Humphrey Wanley et al., *A Catalogue of the Harleian Collection of Manuscripts* (London)
Whatley 1982: Gordon Whatley, 'The Middle English *St Erkenwald* in Its Liturgical Context', *Medievalia* 8, 277–306
— 1984a: 'The Uses of Hagiography: The Legend of Pope Gregory and the Emperor Trajan in the Middle Ages', *Viator* 15, 25–63
— 1984b: '*Piers Plowman* B 12.227–84: Notes on Language, Text and Theology', *MP* 82, 1–12
— 1986: 'Heathens and Saints; *Saint Erkenwald* in Its Legendary Context', *Speculum* 61, 330–63
— 1989: *The Saint of London* (Binghamton, NY)
Yakovlev 2009: Nicolay Yakovlev, 'On Final -*e* in the B-Verses of *Sir Gawain and the Green Knight*', in *Approaches to the Metres of Alliterative Verse*, ed. Judith Jefferson and Ad Putter (Leeds), pp. 135–57
Young 1936: Karl Young, 'Instructions for Parish Priests', *Speculum*, 11, 224–31

Translation, Text and Variants

St Erkenwald

At London in England, not very long ago, after Christ suffered on the cross and established Christianity, there was a bishop in that town, blessed and consecrated; that holy man was called Saint Erkenwald, as I believe. In his time the greatest temple of all in that town was pulled down – a part of it – to rededicate it, for it had been pagan in the days of Hengest, whom the hostile Saxons had sent here. They chased out the Britons and drove them into Wales and corrupted all the people who lived in that country. Then this realm was apostate for many rebellious years until St Augustine was sent by the pope into Sandwich. Then he preached the pure faith here and planted the truth, and converted all the communities to Christianity again. At that time he converted temples that adhered to the Devil, and purified them in the name of Christ, and called them churches. He threw out their idols and brought in saints, and promptly changed their names and placed them under better custody. What was previously Apollo's is now St Peter's, Mahoun's became St Margaret's or Mary Magdalene's, the temple of the Sun was dedicated to Our Lady, Jupiter and Juno to Jesus or James; so whatever had been dedicated to Satan in the time of the Saxons he consecrated and assigned them all to beloved saints. What is now named London was then the New Troy; it has always been the metropolis and the chief city. A mighty devil owned the great minster there, and the temple rights were assigned to his name, for he was honoured as the dearest god among idols

De Erkenwaldo

At London in Englond   no3t full long sythen,
Sythen Crist suffrid on crosse   and Cristendome stablyd,
Ther was a byschop in þat burgh,   blessyd and sacryd;
Saynt Erkenwolde as I hope   þat holy mon hatte.
In his tyme in þat toun   þe temple alder-grattyst   5
Was drawen doun, þat one dole,   to dedifie newe,
For hit hethen had bene   in Hengystes dawes
Þat þe Saxones vnsa3t   haden sende hyder.
Þai bete oute þe Bretons   and bro3t hom into Wales
And peruertyd all þe pepul   þat in þat place dwellid.   10
Þen wos this reame renaide   mony ronke 3eres,
Til Saynt Austyn into Sandewich   was send fro þe pope.
Þen prechyd he here þe pure faythe   and plantyd þe trouthe,
And conuertyd all þe communnates   to Cristendame newe.
He turnyd temples þat tyme   þat temyd to þe deuell,   15
And clansyd hom in Cristes nome   and kyrkes hom callid;
He hurlyd owt hor ydols   and hade hym in sayntes,
And chaungit cheuely hor nomes   and chargit hom better.
Þat ere was of Appolyn   is now of Saynt Petre,
Mahoun to Saynt Margrete   oþir to Maudelayne,   20
Þe synagoge of þe Sonne   was sett to oure Lady,
Jubiter and Jono   to Jesu oþir to James.
So he hom dedifiet and dyght   all to dere halowes
Þat ere wos sett of Sathanas   in Saxones tyme.
Now þat London is neuenyd   hatte þe New Troie,   25
Þe metropol and þe mayster-toun   hit euermore has bene.
Þe mecul mynster þerinne   a maghty deuel aghte,
And þe title of þe temple   bitan was his name,
For he was dryghtyn derrest   of ydols praysid

6 newe] new.   7 Hengystes] Hengyst.   27 aghte] aght.

and the most celebrated in sacrificial rites in Saxon lands. It was regarded as the third temple of the Triapolitans; within all Britain's shores there were only another two.

Now Erkenwald is bishop of Augustine's province at dear London town and teaches the faith, and sits with dignity on the throne of St Paul's minster, which was the Triapolitan temple, as I said before. Then it was demolished and knocked down and rebuilt, a noble construction for its purpose, and it was called 'New Work'. Many a lively mason was set to work there, to hew hard stones with sharp-edged tools, many a digger in the earth to search for solid ground, so that the foundations should support the footings first of all. As they built and excavated they discovered something marvellous, the story of which is still recorded in learned chronicles; for as they worked and dug so deep into the earth, they found a very beautiful tomb constructed on a floor. It was a coffin of solid stone skilfully carved, decorated around with gargoyles all of shining marble. The lid of the tomb that closed it on top was fittingly made of marble and beautifully polished, and the border embellished with bright gold letters. But the words that stood there in a row were mysterious; the letters were entirely distinct, and many studied them there, but all were at a loss as to how to pronounce the inscription and what its meaning might be. Many tonsured clerics in that precinct busied themselves to no purpose to make words out of them.

When news reached the town of the wonderful tomb, many hundreds of worthy citizens hurried there at once; burgesses, town officials and others went there, and many different kinds of craftsmen. Lads left their work and rushed towards that place, ran quickly in a crowd with a resounding noise. So very many of all sorts came there that it was as if the whole world had gathered there on the instant.

And þe solempnest of his sacrifices   in Saxones londes.   30
Þe thrid temple hit wos tolde   of Triapolitanes:
By all Bretaynes bonkes   were bot othire twayne.
    Now of þis Augustynes art   is Erkenwolde bischop
At loue London toun   and the lagh teches,
Syttes semely in þe sege   of Saynt Paule mynster   35
Þat was þe temple Triapolitan   as I tolde are.
Þen was hit abatyd and beten doun   and buggyd efte newe,
A noble note for þe nones   and New Werke hit hatte.
Mony a mery mason   was made þer to wyrke,
Harde stones for to hewe   with eggite toles,   40
Mony grubber in grete   þe grounde for to seche
Þat þe fundement on fyrst   shuld þe fote halde;
And as þai makkyd and mynyd   a meruayle þai founden
As ȝet in crafty cronecles   is kydde þe memorie,
For as þai dyȝt and dalfe   so depe into þe erthe   45
Þai founden fourmyt on a flore   a ferly faire toumbe;
Hit was a throgh of thykke ston   thryuandly hewen,
With gargeles garnysht aboute   alle of gray marbre.
The sperl of þe spelunke   þat spradde hit olofte
Was metely made of þe marbre   and menskefully planed   50
And þe bordure enbelicit   with bryȝt golde lettres;
Bot roynyshe were þe resones   þat þer on row stoden.
Full verray were þe vigures,   þer auisyd hom mony,
Bot all muset hit to mouth   and quat hit mene shulde;
Mony clerke in þat clos   with crownes ful brode   55   fol. 73r
Þer besiet hom aboute noȝt   to bryng hom in wordes.
Quen tithynges token to þe toun   of þe toumbe-wonder,
Mony hundrid hende men   highid þider sone;
Burgeys boghit þerto,   bedels and othire,
And mony a mesters-mon   of maners dyuerse.   60
Laddes laften hor werke   and lepen þiderwardes,
Ronnen radly in route   with ryngande noyce;
Þer commen þider of all kynnes   so kenely mony
Þat as all þe worlde were þider walon   within a honde-quile.

30 Saxones] Saxon.   37 newe] new.   40 eggite] eggit.   49 The] thre.
54 shulde] shuld.   62 ryngande] ryngand.

When the mayor with his retinue saw that marvel, they took charge of the sanctuary with the sacristan's permission, and they ordered the lid to be unfastened and laid to one side; they wanted to look in that casket to see what remained within it.

Strong workmen then went to it, applied levers to it, squeezed them underneath, seized hold by the corners with crowbars of iron and, though the lid was large, they set it aside at once. But then there was great amazement among the people standing around, who could not manage to comprehend an extraordinary marvel, so lovely was the space within, all painted with gold, and a glorious body lay on the bottom, arrayed in an opulent fashion in costly clothes. His gown was hemmed with shining gold, with many precious pearls set on it, and a golden belt encircled his waist, a great mantle above furred with miniver, the fabric of elegant camel-hair with attractive borders, and on his coif was placed a rich crown, and a fine sceptre set in his hand. His clothes were as spotless, without any stain of mould or specks, nor moth-eaten, and their colour as bright in shining hues as if they had been skilfully fashioned yesterday in the precinct. And his face and the bare flesh that showed openly around his ears and hands were as fresh – with a complexion as bright as a rose, and two red lips – as if in good health he had slipped into sleep all of a sudden. There was time spent in vain as each asked the other what body it could be that was buried there. How long had he been lying there, his complexion so unchanged and all his clothing so unspotted? That's what everyone asked. 'A man like that must have been long remembered. He has been king of this country, as seems evident. He lies buried so deep; it's very strange if someone wasn't able to say that he had seen him.'

Quen þe maire with his meynye   þat meruaile aspied,   65
By assent of þe sextene   þe sayntuaré þai kepten,
Bede vnlouke þe lidde   and lay hit byside;
Þai wold loke on þat lome   quat lengyd withinne.
Wyȝt werkemen with þat   wenten þertille,
Putten prises þerto,   pinchid one-vnder,   70
Kaghten by þe corners   with crowes of yrne,
And were þe lydde neuer so large   þai laide hit by sone.
Bot þen wos wonder to wale   on wehes þat stoden
That myȝt not come to to knowe   a quontyse strange,
So was þe glode within gay,   al with golde payntyd,   75
And a blisfull body   opon þe bothum lyggid,
Araide on a riche wise   in rialle wedes.
Al with glisnande golde   his gowne wos hemmyd,
With mony a precious perle   picchit þeronne,
And a gurdill of golde   bigripid his mydell;   80
A meche mantel on lofte   with menyuer furrit,
Þe clothe of camelyn ful clene   with cumely bordures;
And on his coyfe wos kest   a coron ful riche,
And a semely septure   sett in his honde.
Als wemles were his wedes   withouten any tecche   85
Oþir of moulyng, oþir of motes,   oþir moght-freten,
And als bryȝt of hor blee   in blysnande hewes
As þai hade ȝepely in þat ȝorde   bene ȝisturday shapen;
And als freshe hym þe face   and the flesh nakyd
Bi his eres and bi his hondes   þat openly shewid   90
With ronke rode as þe rose   and two rede lippes,
As he in sounde sodanly   were slippid opon slepe.
Þer was spedeles space   to spyr vschon oþir
Quat body hit myȝt be   þat buried wos there;
How long had he þer layne,   his lere so vnchaungit,   95
And al his wede vnwemmyd?   Þus ylka weghe askyd.
'Hit myȝt not be bot such a mon   in mynde stode longe.
He has ben kyng of þis kith,   as couthely hit semes,
He lyes doluen þus depe;   hit is a derfe wonder
Bot summe segge couthe say   þat he hym sene hade.'   100

69 þertille] þertill.   77 rialle] riall.   79 þeronne] þeron.   82 cumely] cumly.
94 there] ther.   97 mynde] myde; longe] long.

But all that fuss was for nothing, for no-one could determine, either from an inscription, or physical evidence, or oral report, that it was ever spoken of in town, or recorded in a book that ever mentioned such a man in any way.

The news was soon brought to the bishop, all the great wonder of the buried body. The primate had travelled away from home with his prelates: Bishop Erkenwald was in Essex visiting an abbey. People related the story to him, together with the disturbance among the people, and such an uproar about a body rang out non-stop that the bishop sent an order by city officers and missives to put an end to it, and then smartly hurried back there on his horse. When he arrived at the illustrious church of St Paul's, many people met him in that place to report the marvel. He passed into his palace and commanded peace, turned aside from the dead body and closed the door after him.

The dark night passed over and the day-bell sounded, and Erkenwald was awake in the dawn before that; almost the whole night he had recited his prayers to beg the Lord, of his sweet grace, to condescend to reveal the mystery to him by a vision or in some other way. 'Though I may be unworthy', he said, weeping, 'let my Lord grant it through his precious grace. In confirmation of thy Christian faith, help me to explain the mystery of this marvel that men are puzzling over.' And for so long did he plead tearfully for grace that he was granted an answer from the Holy Spirit, and then the dawn came.

Minster doors were thrown open when matins were sung, and the bishop prepared himself reverently to sing high mass. The prelate was promptly attired in his episcopal vestments; with his ministers he ceremoniously and in graceful fashion begins the Mass of the Holy Spirit for a successful outcome, with the pleasing sounds of the choir with very elegant notes. Many a richly dressed great lord was gathered to listen to it, since the most noble lords of the realm visit there often, until the service had ended and the closing words spoken; then all the noble company turned from the altar.

Bot þat ilke note wos noght, for nourne none couthe,
Noþir by title ne token ne by tale noþir,
Þat euer wos breuyt in burgh ne in boke notyd
Þat euer mynnyd such a mon, more ne lasse.
    Þe bodeword to þe byschop was broght on a quile   105
Of þat buried body al þe bolde wonder.
Þe primate with his prelacie was partyd fro home,
In Esex was Sir Erkenwolde an abbay to visite.
Tulkes tolden hym þe tale, with troubull in þe pepul,
And suche a cry aboute a cors crakit euermore;   110
The bischop sende hit to blynne by bedels and lettres,   fol. 73v
And buskyd þiderwarde bytyme on his blonke after.
By þat he come to þe kyrke kydde of Saynt Paule,
Mony hym metten on þat meere þe meruayle to telle.
He passyd into his palais and pes he comaundit   115
And deuoydit fro þe dede and ditte þe durre after.
Þe derke ny3t ouerdrofe and day-belle ronge,
And Sir Erkenwolde was vp in þe vghten ere þenne,
Þat welnegh al þe ny3t hade naytyd his houres
To biseche his Souerayn, of his swete grace,   120
To vouchesafe to reuele hym hit by a visoun or elles.
'Þagh I be vnworthi,' al wepand he sayde,
'Thurgh his deere debonerté digne hit my Lorde:
In confirmyng þi Cristen faith, fulsen me to kenne
Þe mysterie of þis meruaile þat men opon wondres.'   125
And so long he grette after grace þat he graunte hade,
An ansuare of þe Holy Goste, and afterwarde hit dawid.
Mynster-dores were makyd opon quen matens were songen,
Þe byschop hym shope solemply to synge þe hegh masse.
Þe prelate in pontificals was prestly atyrid,   130
Manerly with his ministres þe masse he begynnes
Of *Spiritus Domini* for his spede, opon sutile wise,
With queme questis of þe quere with ful quaynt notes.
Mony a gay grete lorde was gedrid to herken hit,
As þe rekenest of þe reame repairen þider ofte,   135
Till cessyd was þe seruice and sayde þe later ende;
Þen heldyt fro þe autere all þe hegh gynge.

103 boke] boko. 104 mon] more. 114 telle] tell. 118 þenne] þen. 119 naytyd] nattyd. 132 opon] on.

The prelate crossed the floor where lords bowed to him; richly vested as he was, he went up to the tomb. Men with bunches of keys opened the enclosure to him, but there was a crush among the great crowd that followed him. The bishop came to the burial place with barons beside him, the mayor with many important men and mace-bearers before him. The dean of the honoured place gave an account of everything right away, and pointed with his finger to the discovery of the marvel. 'Look, lords', said that man, 'this body here has been lying enclosed down below, it's not known for how long; and yet his colour and his clothing have received no damage, nor has his flesh, nor the coffin that he has been lying in. There's no man alive of such great age as to be able to recall to mind that such a man ruled, nor to say a single word about his name nor his occupation. Yet many a poorer man is interred in this place whose memory is recorded in our burial register for all time. And we've searched our library for seven whole days, but we couldn't ever find a single chronicle account of this king. To judge from physical indications, he hasn't been lying here so long as to vanish entirely from memory, unless something extraordinary has happened.'

'What you say is true', said the man who was consecrated as bishop. 'It is a marvel to men that amounts to little in relation to the divine wisdom of the Prince who rules Paradise, when he chooses to unlock the least of his powers. But when man's power is defeated and his mind surpassed, and all his faculties are torn to shreds and he stands baffled, then it causes God very little trouble to set free with a finger what all the hands on earth could never hold. In a situation where the capacity of created beings deviates from understanding, the support of the Creator must undertake the remedy. And so let us get on with our business and speculate no further. You see there's no use in seeking the truth among ourselves, but let us all call upon God and ask for his grace, for he's ungrudging in sending counsel and support, and he does that in order to confirm your faith and true belief. I'll so convincingly inform you of his powers that finally you'll be able to believe that he is Lord Almighty, and ready to fulfil your desires if you trust him as your friend.'

Þe prelate passid on þe playn,   þer plied to hym lordes,
As riche reuestid as he was   he rayked to þe toumbe;
Men vnclosid hym þe cloyster   with clustrede keies,   140
Bot pyne wos with þe grete prece   þat passyd hym after.
The byschop come to þe burynes,   him barones besyde,
Þe maire with mony maȝti men   and macers before hym.
Þe dene of þe dere place   deuysit al on fyrste,
Þe fyndynge of þat ferly   with fynger he mynte.   145
'Lo, lordes,' quod þat lede,   'suche a lyche here is
Has layn loken here on logh,   how long is vnknawen;
And ȝet his colour and his clothe   has caȝt no defaute,
Ne his lire, ne þe lome   þat he is layde inne.
Þer is no lede opon lyfe   of so long age   150
Þat may mene in his mynde   þat suche a mon regnyd,
Ne noþir his nome ne his note   nourne of one speche;
Queþer mony porer in þis place   is putte into graue
Þat merkid is in oure martilage   his mynde for euer;
And we haue oure librarie laitid   þes long seuen dayes,   155
Bot one cronicle of þis kyng   con we neuer fynde.
He has non layne here so long,   to loke hit by kynde,
To malte so out of memorie   bot meruayle hit were.'
'Þou says soþe,' quod þe segge   þat sacrid was byschop,
'Hit is meruaile to men,   þat mountes to litell   160
Toward þe prouidens of þe prince   þat paradis weldes
Quen hym luste to vnlouke   þe leste of his myȝtes.
Bot quen matyd is monnes myȝt   and his mynde passyd,
And al his resons are torent   and redeles he stondes,
Þen lettes hit hym ful litell   to louse wyt a fynger   165
Þat all þe hondes vnder heuen   halde myȝt neuer.
Þereas creatures crafte   of counsell oute swarues,   fol. 74r
Þe comforth of þe creatore   byhoues þe cure take.
And so do we now oure dede,   deuyne we no fyrre;
To seche þe soth at oureselfe   ȝee se þer no bote,   170
Bot glow we all opon Godde   and his grace aske,
Þat careles is of counsell   and comforthe to sende,
And þat in fastynge of ȝour faith   and of fyne bileue.
I shal auay ȝow so verrayly   of vertues hise
Þat ȝe may leue vpon long   þat he is lord myȝty   175
And fayne ȝour talent to fulfille   if ȝe hym frende leues.'

140 clustrede] clustred.   144 fyrste] fyrst.   174 hise] his.

Then he turns to the tomb and addresses the body. Lifting his eyes, he spoke these words: 'Now body that lies there, remain silent no longer. Since Jesus has decided today that his joy should be manifested, be obedient to his bidding, I command you on his behalf. As he was stretched on a beam when he shed his blood, as you know for certain, and we firmly believe it, answer my words here; conceal none of the truth! Since we don't know who you are, tell us yourself what man you were in the world and why you are lying like this, how long you have been lying here and what religion you practised, and whether you are assigned to joy or condemned to torment.'

When the man had spoken in this way and then sighed, the fair body in the tomb stirred a little, and with a mournful voice utters words through some spirit-life granted by him who governs life. 'Bishop', said this body, 'your command is welcome to me; I couldn't refuse to submit to your request for anything in the world. All heaven and hell, and earth in between them, bow to the name that you've spoken and by which you've addressed me. First, to tell you the truth of who I was: quite the most unfortunate man who ever walked on earth; never a king or emperor, nor even a knight, but a lawyer who lived in this land then. I was appointed and made a chief official here to preside in court cases; I governed this city under a high-ranking prince of pagan faith, and everyone who followed him held the same belief. The length of my lying here is an unknown period of time, it is too great for anyone to calculate; after Brutus had originally built this town, just eighteen years short of five hundred before your Christ was born by Christian reckoning: that is a thousand years and thirty more plus three times eight. I was an inheritor of affliction in New Troy in the reign of the noble king who ruled us then:

Then he turnes to þe toumbe   and talkes to þe corce,
Lyftand vp his egh-lyddes   he loused such wordes:
'Now, lykhame þat þou lies,   layne þou no lenger!
Sythen Jesus has iuggit today   his ioy to be schewyd,   180
Be þou bone to his bode,   I bydde in his behalue.
As he was bende on a beme   quen he his blode schedde,
As þou hit wost wyterly   and we hit wele leuen,
Ansuare here to my sawe,   councele no trouthe!
Sithen we wot not qwo þou art,   witere vs þiselwen   185
In worlde quat weghe þou was   and quy þow þus ligges,
How long þou has layne here   and quat lagh þou vsyt,
Queþer art þou ioyned to ioy   or iuggid to pyne.'
Quen þe segge hade þus sayde   and syked þerafter,
Þe bryȝt body in þe burynes   brayed a litell,   190
And with a drery dreme   he dryues owte wordes
Þurgh sum lant goste-lyfe   of hym þat lyfe redes.
'Bisshop,' quod þis ilke body,   'þi boode is me dere;
I may not bot bogh to þi bone   for bothe myn eghen.
To þe name þat þou neuenyd has   and nournet me after   195
Al heuen and helle heldes to   and erthe bitwene.
Fyrst to say the þe sothe   quo myselfe were:
One þe vnhapnest hathel   þat euer on erth ȝode,
Neuer kyng ne cayser   ne ȝet no knyȝt nothyre,
Bot a lede of þe lagh   þat þen þis londe vsit.   200
I was committid and made   a mayster-mon here
To sytte vpon sayd causes;   þis cité I ȝemyd
Vnder a prince of parage   of paynymes laghe,
And vche segge þat him sewid   þe same fayth trowid.
Þe lengthe of my lying here,   þat is a lewid date,   205
Hit is to meche to any mon   to make of a nombre.
After þat Brutus þis burgh   had buggid on fyrste,
Noȝt bot fife hundred ȝere   þer aghtene wontyd
Before þat kynned ȝour Criste   by Cristen acounte –
A þousand ȝere and þritty mo   and ȝet threnen aghte.   210
I was an heire of anoye   in þe New Troie
In þe regne of þe riche kyng   þat rewlit vs þenne,

185 wot] *last two letters obscured by stain;* þiselwen] w *blotted.*   186 weghe] w *partly obscured by stain.*   188 or] oþir.   192 lyfe (2)] al.   203 laghe] lagh. 206 is] *omitted.*   210 aghte] aght.   212 þenne] þen.

the fearless Briton Sir Belinus; his brother was Sir Brennius. Bitter was the abuse exchanged between them because of their vengeful war while their anger lasted. At that time I was appointed a judge here in the pagan law.'

While he spoke in the tomb thus, there arose among the people no word anywhere at all, and no noise broke out, but all stood as still as stone and listened, seized with great amazement, and many wept. The bishop commands the body: 'Explain the reason, since you were not recognised as a king, why you wear the crown. Why do you hold the sceptre so high in your hand, since you possessed no land with vassals, and no power over life or limb?'

'Dear sir', said the dead body, 'I intend to explain it to you, even though it was never by my wish that it should have been arranged in this way. I was a deputy and a judge under a noble duke, and this place was put entirely under my jurisdiction. I administered justice in this lovely town according to pagan law, and always in accord with good faith, for more than forty years. The people were treacherous and corrupt and unruly to control; I often suffered harm to keep them to what is right; but not for danger, nor for riches, nor hostility nor fear, nor for force, nor for reward, nor for awe of any man, did I ever depart from what was right, according to my own judgement, to deliver a false decision on any day of my life. My conscience never turned aside for worldly avarice to make false judgements in a dishonest decision. However powerful a man, out of deference, nor for anyone's threat, nor trouble or pity, no-one persuaded me to swerve from the true path of justice, in so far as my faith conformed to my conscience. Though he had been my father's murderer, I offered him no wrongs, nor offered false favour to my father, even if it resulted in him being hanged. And because I was just and upright and versed in the law, when I died all Troy resounded with mourning. All lamented my death, the rich and the poor, and so in my honour they buried my body in gold,

The bolde Breton Sir Belyn   – Sir Berynge was his brothire;
Bitter was þe busmare   boden hom bitwene
For hor wrakeful werre   quil hor wrath lastyd.   215
Þen was I iuge here enioynyd   in gentile lawe.'
    Quil he in spelunke þus spake,   þer sprange in þe pepull
In al þis worlde no worde,   ne wakenyd no noice,
Bot al as stille as þe ston   stoden and listonde,
With meche wonder forwrast,   and wepid ful mony.   220
    The bisshop biddes þat body: 'Biknowe þe cause,
Sithen þou was kidde for no kynge,   quy þou þe croun weres.
Quy haldes þou so hegh   in honde þe septre
And hades no londe of lege men,   ne life ne lym aghtes?'
'Dere sir,' quod þe dede body,   'deuyse þe I thenke,   225   fol. 74v
Al was hit neuer my wille   þat wroght þus hit were.
I wos deputate and domesmon   vnder a duke noble,
And in my power þis place   was putte altogeder.
I iustifiet þis ioly toun   on gentile wise,
And euer in fourme of gode faithe,   more þen fourty wynter.   230
Þe folke was felonse and fals   and frowarde to reule –
I hent harmes ful ofte   to holde hom to ri3te;
Bot for wothe ne wele,   ne wrathe ne drede,
Ne for maystrie ne for mede,   ne for no monnes aghe,
I remewit neuer fro þe ri3t,   by reson myn awen,   235
For to dresse a wrang dome   no day of my lyue,
Declynet neuer my consciens   for couetise on erthe
In no gynful iugement   no iapes to make.
Were a renke neuer so riche,   for reuerens sake,
Ne for no monnes manas,   ne meschefe ne routhe,   240
Non gete me fro þe hegh gate   to glent out of ry3te
Als ferforthe as my faith   confourmyd my herte.
Þagh had bene my fader bone,   I bede hym no wranges,
Ne fals fauour to my fader,   þagh fell hym be hongyt.
And for I was ry3twis and reken   and redy of þe laghe,   245
Quen I deghed for dul   denyed all Troye;
Alle menyd my morte,   þe more and the lasse,
And þus to bounty my body   þai buriet in golde,

214 Bitter] Mony one.   216 gentile] gentil.   229 gentile] gentil.   232 ri3te] ri3t.   241 ri3te] ri3t.   242 herte] hert.   247 morte] dethe.

dressed me as the most gracious who presided over the lawcourt, in a mantle as the most compassionate and humane on the judge's seat, girdled me as the governor and most eminent of Troy, decked me with fur as the most perfect of inner loyalty. In honour of my honesty of the highest distinction, they crowned me the acknowledged king of wise judges who was ever enthroned in Troy or was believed ever would be; and for I always rewarded what was right, they gave me the sceptre.'

The bishop asks him further, with sorrow in his heart, even though he was honoured in this way, how it could be that his clothes were so unblemished. 'It seems to me they should have rotted into shreds and been torn into tatters long ago. Your body may be embalmed; it doesn't puzzle me that no rot or foul maggots may touch it. But your clothing and its colour – I don't know any way that it might lie and last so long by human skill.'

'No, bishop', the body said, 'I was never embalmed, nor has any human skill kept my clothes unblemished, but it was the noble King of Justice who always rewards righteousness and sincerely loves all the practises that are consistent with what is right; and most of all he honours those who observe justice more than for all the praiseworthy deeds that people perform in the world; and if people have dressed me like this on account of my justice, he who loves justice most has granted that I may endure'.

'Yes, but what do you have to say of your soul?' said the bishop then. 'Where is she settled and placed, if you acted so correctly? He who rewards each person as he has justly deserved could hardly fail to give you some share of his grace; for as he says in his true writings in the Psalms: "The just and the innocent always hasten to me." Therefore tell me of your soul, where she dwells in bliss, and of the rich redemption that Our Lord has granted her.'

Then he who lay there murmured and shook his head, and gave a great groan, and said to God: 'Mighty creator of men, your powers are great: how might your mercy ever be sufficient for me?

Cladden me for þe curtest   þat courte couthe þen holde,
In mantel for þe mekest   and monlokest on benche,   250
Gurden me for þe gouernour   and graythist of Troie,
Furrid me for þe fynest   of faith me withinne.
For þe honour of myn honesté   of heghest enprise
Þai coronyd me þe kidde kynge   of kene iustises
Þer euer wos tronyd in Troye   or trowid euer shulde,   255
And for I rewardid euer riȝt   þai raght me the septre.'
    Þe bisshop baythes hym ȝet,   with bale at his herte,
Þagh men menskid him so,   how hit myȝt worthe
Þat his clothes were so clene.   'In cloutes, me thynkes,
Hom burde haue rotid and bene rent   in rattes long sythen.   260
Þi body may be enbawmyd,   hit bashis me noght
Þat hit thar ryne no rote   ne no ronke wormes;
Bot þi coloure ne þi clothe   – I know in no wise
How hit myȝt lye by monnes lore   and laste so longe.'
    'Nay, bisshop,' quod þat body,   'enbawmyd wos I neuer,   265
Ne no monnes counsell my cloth   has kepyd vnwemmyd,
Bot þe riche kyng of reson,   þat riȝt euer alowes
And loues al þe lawes lely   þat longen to trouthe;
And moste he menskes men   for mynnyng of riȝtes
Þen for al þe meritorie medes   þat men on molde vsen;   270
And if renkes for riȝt   þus me arayed haue,
He has lant me to last   þat loues ryȝt best.'
    'Ȝea, bot sayes þou of þi saule,'   þen sayde þe bisshop;
'Quere is ho stablid and stadde,   if þou so streȝt wroghtes?
He þat rewardes vche a renke   as he has riȝt seruyd   275
Myȝt euel forgo the to gyfe   of his grace summe brawnche.
For as he says in his sothe   psalmyde writtes:
"Þe skilfulle and þe vnskathely   skelton ay to me."
Forþi say me of þi soule,   in sele quere ho wonnes,
And of þe riche restorment   þat raȝt hyr oure Lorde.'   280
Þen hummyd he þat þer lay   and his hedde waggyd,
And gefe a gronyng ful grete,   and to Godde sayde:
'Maȝty maker of men,   thi myghtes are grete;
How myȝt þi mercy to me   amounte any tyme?

255 or] oþir. 257 herte] hert. 262 no (1)] ne. 264 laste] last. 271 haue] has. 273 sayde] sayd.

Was I not a pagan, unprepared, who never knew your covenant, nor the extent of your mercy, nor your great power, but I was always a person without faith, who failed in your laws in which you, Lord, were always glorified? Alas, the hard times! I was not numbered among those whom you redeemed with suffering, with the blood from your body upon the dark cross. When you harrowed the pit of hell and took those remaining out of limbo, you left me there, and there sits my soul who can see no further, languishing in the dark death to which our father Adam condemned us, our ancestor who ate from the apple that has poisoned many blameless people for ever. You were poisoned by his teeth and you consume the filth, but you are restored to life when cured by a medicine: that is baptism in the font with faithful belief, and my soul and I, unforgiven, have not received that. What did we who always acted justly gain by our good deeds, when we are miserably condemned into the deep pit, and so exiled from that supper, that sacred feast, where those that hungered after justice are richly refreshed? My soul may sit there in sorrow and sigh bitterly, miserably in that dark death where morning never dawns, hungry in hell-pit, and look out for meals for a long time before she may see that supper or anyone to invite her to it.'

Thus did this dead body miserably describe its sorrow, so that all who heard the words wept for sadness, and the bishop lowered his eyes in distress. So copious were his sobs that he had no moment to speak, until he took an opportunity and in floods of tears looked towards the tomb, to the body that lay there. 'May Our Lord grant', said the bishop, 'that you had life, with God's leave, for as long as I might fetch water and cast it on your fair body and speak these words: "I baptise thee in the name of the Father and of his noble Child, and of the gracious Holy Spirit", and not one moment longer; then if you dropped down dead it would affect me less.'

Nas I a paynym vnpreste,   þat neuer thi plite knewe,   285 fol. 75r
Ne þe mesure of þi mercy   ne þi mecul vertue,
Bot ay a freke faitheles   þat faylid þi laghes
Þat euer þou, Lord, wos louyd in?   Allas þe harde stoundes!
I was non of þe nommbre   þat þou with noy boghtes
With þe blode of thi body   vpon þe blo rode.   290
Quen þou herghdes helle-hole   and hentes hom þeroute,
Þi loffynge oute of limbo,   þou laftes me þere,
And þer sittes my soule   þat se may no fyrre,
Dwynande in þe derke deth   þat dyȝt vs oure fader,
Adam oure alder,   þat ete of þat appull   295
Þat mony a plyȝtles pepul   has poysned for euer.
Ȝe were entouchid with his tethe   and take in þe glotte,
Bot mendyd with a medecyn   ȝe are made for to lyuye –
Þat is fulloght in fonte   with faitheful bileue,
And þat han we myste alle merciles,   myselfe and my soule.   300
Quat wan we with oure wele dede   þat wroghtyn ay riȝte,
Quen we are dampnyd dulfully   into þe depe lake,
And exilid fro þat soper so,   þat solempne feste,
Þer richely hit arne refetyd   þat after right hungride?
My soule may sitte þer in sorow   and sike ful colde,   305
Dymly in þat derke dethe   þer dawes neuer morowen,
Hungrie inwith helle-hole,   and herken after meeles,
Longe er ho þat soper se   or segge hyr to lathe.'
    Þus dulfully þis dede body   deuisyt hit sorowe
Þat alle wepyd for woo   þe wordes þat herden,   310
And þe bysshop balefully   bere doun his eghen,
Þat hade no space to speke,   so spakly he ȝoskyd,
Til he toke hym a tome   and to þe toumbe lokyd
To þe liche þer hit lay,   with lauande teres.
'Oure Lord lene', quod þat lede,   'þat þou lyfe hades,   315
By Goddes leue, as longe   as I myȝt lacche water,
And cast vpon þi faire cors   and carpe þes wordes,
"I folwe þe in þe Fader nome   and his fre Childes
And of þe gracious Holy Goste",   and not one grue lenger.
Þen þof þou droppyd doun dede,   hit daungerde me lasse.'   320

286 þe] þi.   292 me þere] ne þer.   301 riȝte] riȝt.   302 depe] d *blotted*.
303 feste] fest.   306 Dymly] dynly.   308 or] oþir.

With the words that he uttered, the water from his eyes and the tears rolled down and landed on the tomb, and one fell on the man's face, and he sighed, and then said in a reverent voice: 'Blessed be Our Saviour! Now praise be to you, high God, and your gracious mother, and blessed be the joyous hour in which she bore you! And also praise be to you, bishop, the remedy for my sorrow and the release from the awful privations in which my soul has lived! For the words that you uttered and the water that you shed, the shining stream from your eyes, has brought about my baptism. The first splash that fell on me cured all my pain. Just now my soul is seated at the table at supper, for with the words and the water that washed us of suffering, a gleam flashed brightly low in the abyss, so that my spirit sprang quickly with unrestrained joy, ceremoniously into the room where all the faithful dine, and there a steward met her with the greatest honour, and with deference he granted her a place forever. For that I praise my high God, and also you, bishop, who has brought us from sorrow to bliss, blessed be you!'

With that his voice ceased. He said no more, but suddenly his sweet face faded away and vanished, and all the colour of his body became as black as earth, as decayed as rotten stuff that rises in dust. For as soon as the soul was established in bliss, that other matter that covered the bones decayed; for that everlasting life that will never end banishes every vanity that serves so little purpose. Then was there praise of our Lord with hands uplifted, much sorrow and joy were mingled together. They passed forth in procession and all the people followed, and all the bells in the town rang out in unison.

With þat worde þat he warpyd,   þe wete of his eghen
And teres trillyd adoun   and on þe toumbe lighten,
And one felle on his face,   and þe freke syked.
Þen sayd he with a sadde soun: 'Oure Sauyoure be louyd!
Now herid be þou, hegh God,   and þi hende Moder,   325
And blissid be þat blisful houre   þat ho the bere inne!
And also be þou, bysshop,   þe bote of my sorowe
And þe relefe of þe lodely lures   þat my soule has leuyd inne!
For þe wordes þat þou werpe   and water þat þou sheddes,
Þe bryȝt bourne of þin eghen,   my bapteme is worthyn.   330
Þe fyrst slent þat on me slode   slekkyd al my tene.
Ryȝt now to soper my soule   is sette at þe table;
For with þe wordes and þe water   þat wesche vs of payne,
Liȝtly lasshit þer a leme   loghe in þe abyme,
Þat spakly sprent my spyryt   with vnsparid murthe   335
Into þe cenacle solemply   þer soupen all trewe;
And þer a marciall hyr mette   with menske alder-grattest,
And with reuerence a rowme   he raȝt hyr for euer.
I heere þerof my hegh God   and also þe, bysshop,
Fro bale has broȝt vs to blis,   blessid þou worthe!'   340
                                                            fol. 75v
   Wyt this cessyd his sowne,   sayd he no more,
Bot sodenly his swete chere   swyndid and faylid
And all the blee of his body   wos blakke as þe moldes,
As roten as þe rottok   þat rises in powdere.
For as sone as þe soule   was sesyd in blisse,   345
Corrupt was þat oþir crafte   þat couert þe bones;
For þe ay-lastande life   þat lethe shall neuer
Deuoydes vche a vayneglorie   þat vayles so litelle.
Þen wos louyng oure Lord   with loves vphalden,
Meche mournyng and myrthe   was mellyd togeder.   350
Þai passyd forthe in procession   and alle þe pepull folowid,
And all þe belles in þe burgh   beryd at ones.

321 of his] of *followed by space.* 326 inne] in. 328 inne] in. 329 water] þe water. 336 trewe] trew. 340 worthe] worth.

Annotations

1–32 Like *Wynnere* and *Gawain*, the poem opens with a 'historical' prologue alluding to Geoffrey of Monmouth's account of the ancient Britons, though much of the information here is more truly historical and relies on Bede. See Introduction pp. 19–22 on the sources. *St Erkenwald* begins with a precise definition of space, at London in England, and a slippery statement of time. The prominent double *siþen* linking the first two lines, 'not all that long ago, after Christ suffered', compresses the gap between the poet's audience and Erkenwald, bishop of London from 675 until his death in 693, temporally seven centuries apart, and it links the bishop with Christ, also seven centuries apart, doing Christ's work re-establishing the faith in London. Furthermore, Erkenwald is seen as continuing and completing the work of Augustine, demolishing and rededicating St Paul's after Augustine had preached the true faith and converted the people to Christianity. In fact Augustine had arrived in Britain almost a century before, in 597, and Bede names and dates the three bishops of London, Mellitus, Cedd and Wini, who followed him and preceded Erkenwald. The poet moves from AD 33 to 675 and back to 597, interposing between Erkenwald and Augustine a fourth event, the arrival of the Saxons led by Hengist, which, according to Bede, took place at the invitation of Vortigern in 447. And so from the *Saxones tyme* we come to *Now* in London (25 and 33). All of this relies on Bede, with the difference that Bede is meticulous about dates, such as Pope Gregory's instructions to Augustine to travel to Britain, 'given on the 23 July, in the fourteenth year of the reign of the our most religious emperor Maurice Tiberius, and the thirteenth year after his consulship', i.e. 596 (i.22). Bede's history is concerned with actual rather than symbolic time.

1 *in Englond*: the Palatinate of Cheshire was in many respects separate from the rest of England. See Introduction, p. 13, and Burrow 1993. For *long sythen*, 'a long time ago', see l. 260.

6 *þat one dole*: 'a part of it'. This rebuilding is the *New Werke* (38).

7–8 Bede relates that the pagan Saxons invaded, led by Hengist and Horsa, who ravaged the cities and countryside (Bede i.15).

8 *vnsaȝt*: 'hostile, warlike', though also suggesting hostility towards God; cf. (of believers in witchcraft) 'Swych beyn þe deuyl betaght / With holy church þey ben vnsaght' (Mannyng, *Handlyng Synne* 481–2). From *saught*, 'reconciliation', as in *Pearl* 1201, *sete saȝt*, 'made reconciliation' (with God).

9 'Such Britons as remained sought refuge in the western parts of the kingdom: that is, in Cornwall and Wales' (Geoffrey xi.10), followed by Chaucer: 'To Walys fledde the Cristyanytee / Of olde Britons dwellynge in this ile' (*CT* II.544–5).

10 *peruertyd*: 'led from the true faith'; resolved by *conuertyd* (14).

11 *renaide*: 'apostate', having abandoned the Christianity established by King Lucius in AD 156 (Bede i.4). There was a further relapse shortly before Erkenwald's episcopate in 665; see Bede iii.30.

ronke: 'rebellious'; the adjective (modern *rank*) has a huge range of senses, good and bad; cf. ll. 91, 262. For the sense here, cf. 'þe rauen so ronk þat rebel watz euer' (*Cleanness* 455).

12 In 597 Augustine and his companions, sent by Pope Gregory to convert the Anglo-Saxons, landed on the Isle of Thanet, then separated from the mainland of Kent, as described by Bede (i.25). In the poet's time Sandwich was one of the cinque ports on the mainland nearby. Augustine became archbishop of Canterbury and in 601 appointed Mellitus as first bishop of London.

15–18 Geoffrey reports that at the first christianisation of Britain in AD 156 the converts rededicated 'the temples which had been founded in honour of a multiplicity of gods' (iv.19). Similarly, at the second conversion Pope Gregory wrote to Mellitus to pass on to Augustine lengthy instructions, including the command that pagan temples should not be destroyed but sprinkled with holy water and 'changed from the worship of devils to the service of the true God' (Bede i.30).

18 *chargit*: Both noun and verb have a wide range of senses; see *MED charge* and *chargen*, though this instance is not cited. In context the phrase probably means 'placed them (the temples) in better custody', by rededicating them to patron saints. Cf. *OED charge* n. 13 a. At the first

conversion, says Geoffrey (5.i), Lucius 'turned to better use [in meliorem usum vertens] the goods and the lands which the idolatrous temples had hitherto owned'.

19 *Appolyn*: In a famous episode Geoffrey of Monmouth relates how the Saxon leader Hengist explains to the British king Vortigern that Saxons worship Saturn, Jupiter and especially Mercury, called Woden in their language, after whom Wednesday is named, and Freia, the most powerful goddess, who gives her name to Friday (Geoffrey vi.10). To this list Wace adds Phoebus (*Roman de Brut* 6773-80). Laȝamon expands the list considerably, naming Apollo and Tervagaunt (on whom see *OED termagant*) as well as the gods celebrated in the other days of the week (*Brut* 6935-55). The poet would have learnt of British worship of Apollo from Geoffrey's amusing story of how king Bladud 'constructed a pair of wings for himself and tried to fly through the upper air. He came down on top of the Temple of Apollo in Trinovantium', i.e. London (Geoffrey ii.10). Laȝamon (*Brut* 1434-46) gives a dramatic account of Bladud's death.

20 *Mahoun*: A form of Mahomet, used as the name of a pagan God of any denomination, especially in the romances. In *Sir Bevis of Hampton* a Saracen tells Bevis to 'honour thy god, as y do myne, / Both Mahounde and Apolyn' (cited by *MED Mahoun*). In his account of the cleansing of the temples at the first conversion Laȝamon reports that statues of Mahoun were dragged out by hands and feet and burnt in dark fires (*Brut* 5079-80).

21 *synagoge of þe Sonne*: In his remarkable account of the excavations at St Alban's, Matthew Paris reports that the ancient British inhabitants of 'Werlamcester' especially worshipped Phoebus, god of the sun (*Gesta Abbatum Monasterii Sancti Albani*, i. 26-8). *Synagoge* does not here refer specifically to a Jewish place of worship. In *Wars* 1182 Alexander visits a *synagoge* to worship Ammon.

22 *Jubiter*: On his journey to Britain Brutus stops off at the temple of Diana to set up altars to Jupiter, Diana and Mercury (Geoffrey i.11).

25 *New Troie*: From Geoffrey i.17. For the resonances of the name in the fourteenth century see Turner 2009, pp. 56-92, with a discussion of *St Erkenwald* on pp. 64-71.

27 Perhaps Woden is implied here. Referring to King Bladud's fall, Laȝamon says: 'I Lundene stod / Appollones temple, þe wes þe tirfulle Feond', i.e. 'the mighty Devil' (*Brut* 1444-5).

28 *title*: 'a legal right to the possession of land or immovable property' (*MED title* 6 (a)). For this sense see *Piers Plowman* C.20.324: 'We haen no trewe title to hem'. The mighty devil *aghte*, 'owned, possessed', the temple that later became St Paul's Minster.

31 'It was reckoned as the third Triapolitan temple'. At the first conversion the three pagan *archiflamines*, 'high priests', in London, York and Caerleon, were replaced by three archbishops (Geoffrey iv.19). *Triapolitanes*, not elsewhere recorded, is presumably based on *metropolitan* (cf. *metropol* 26) which may refer to both an archbishop and a chief city (*MED metropolitan(e* n. 1 (a) and (b)), with the substitution of the prefix *tria-* (*MED tri-*), 'three'.

33 *art*: contextually 'province', a sense developed from *OED airt*, 'a quarter of the heavens; a direction. Hence more generally: a quarter, a locality'; *MED art* n. (2). Common in Scottish texts, and probably of Celtic origin; see Breeze 2008. Augustine's province as archbishop of Canterbury at first included London, and in 601 Pope Gregory instructed him to appoint twelve bishops, including bishops of York and London (Bede i. 31-2). In this way the poet defines Erkenwald as a successor to Augustine in his proselytising role teaching the *lagh*, 'faith', on which see l. 124.

37 *MED abaten* 1a (a) quotes Mandeville: 'Ierusalem hath … ben destroyed & the walles abated & beten doun'.

38 Cf. 'Mony noble for þe nonest to þe note yode' (*DT* 284). The phrase 'for þe nones', often used loosely as an intensive, here has its full sense 'for the purpose or occasion', and *note* (*MED note* n. (2), 2(f)) means here 'piece of work, structure', as in *Pearl* 922, referring to the heavenly city. Cf. 101n, 152n.

New Werke: In 1633 Henry Holland recorded an inscription beside Erkenwald's shrine stating that he had enlarged St Paul's: 'novis ædificijs auxit' (Holland 1633, fol. F). In 1603 John Stow wrote: 'The new worke of Powls (so called) at the East end aboue the Quire, was begun in the year 1251' (Stow 1908, 1.326). Of course, previous constructions may also have been known as New Work. The earlier St Paul's was destroyed by a fire in 1087 and the rebuilding was interrupted by another fire in 1135.

39-42 In *Siege* Titus orders the walls of Jerusalem to be undermined: 'With mynours and masouns myne þey bygonne, / Grobben faste on þe grounde' (1110-11). Both *mason* and *grubber* are occupational terms, recorded as surnames by *MED masoun* and *grubbere*. Perhaps 'made þer to wyrke' refers to the practice of impressing masons, as described by Shelby 1964, 387–403. The *grounde* is the substratum supporting the *fundement*, foundations, on which are laid the *fote*, the base or footing of the walls. *MED foundement* 1(a); *fot* 4(b).

44 The poet prefaces his meticulous description of the tomb with the claim that its discovery is a matter of historical record. See Turville-Petre 2005, 362–3. There is a direct contrast with the lack of record for the corpse, l. 156.

46–52 The precise depiction of the tomb has no parallel; see Turville-Petre 2018, pp. 99–103. It is decorated with *gargeles* of grey marble: the word 'gargoyles' referring elsewhere to grotesque water spouts (from French probably from a Spanish word for 'throat') occurs earlier in England only in Latin building accounts (*MED gargoile*). There are mysterious characters around the border that no-one can read. These *resones*, 'inscribed letters' (*MED resoun* 9a), are *roynyshe*, an adjective found elsewhere only in the poems of the *Gawain* poet. The words inscribed on the wall at Belshazzar's feast are *runisch*, 'mysterious' or 'indecipherable' (*Cleanness* 1545). In Laȝamon's *Brut* the OE compound *rūn-stæf* retains the sense 'runic symbol': 'He lette þer-on grauen sælcuðe run-stauen / Hu he Rodric of-sloh' (4967–8). 'He had strange runic letters engraved on it, how he slew Rodric'; see *MED roun* n. (2), and it is possible that the sense 'runic' survives in the adjective here. In 1852 workmen unearthed a Viking gravestone in St Paul's churchyard. Around the rim it has runic characters, and on the face is carved the 'Great Beast'. For 'St Paul's Runestone' see Barnes and Page 2006, pp. 285–8 and plates 74–5. Perhaps the poet had seen this or a similar stone to provide the basis of his description.

47 *thryuandly*: formed on 'thrive'; both the adv. and adj. *thriuande* are recorded almost exclusively in alliterative verse; see *MED thriven*, *thrivingly*; *OED thriving* and *thrivingly*. For the adv. see *Gawain* 1080, 1380, and *Wars* 3875; for the adj. *Gawain* 1980, *Cleanness* 751, and especially *DT* 17x, usually in the phrase ~ *in armys*. For discussion of senses see Clark 1951, 390–1. Here some such sense as 'gracefully' or 'skilfully' is appropriate. The gloss in the ms. is 'artificialy'.

48 *gray* refers as much to the shininess of the marble as to the colour. For the combination see *Wars* 1453, 4592; *MED grei* 2 (a).

49 A *sperl* is something that locks or fastens, such as a bolt, related to MDu *sperrelen*. It is used of the great stone rolled across the entrance of Christ's

tomb (see *MED sperel*). Here it refers to the marble lid of the tomb. The verb *spradde* is either an error for *sparde* or a metathesised form.

53 *verray*, 'distinct', contrasts with *roynyshe*: the shapes of the letters were plain enough, but their meaning was mysterious.

54 *muset hit to mouth*: 'wondered how to pronounce it': *mouth* is a verb.

55 *clos*: St Paul's close 'had a crenellated wall round it, with gates and posterns' (Schofield 2011, p. 161).

crownes: 'tonsures' (*MED coroune* 11). Though able to read Latin, the clerics were unable to make words of the mysterious letters, and in fact their meaning is never revealed. In a similar situation, the learned clerics summoned by Balthazar to interpret the writing on the wall are quite unable to do so: 'alle þat loked on þat letter, as lewed þay were / As þay had loked in þe leþer of my lyft bote' (*Cleanness* 1580–1).

57 *token to*: 'extended to, reached' (*MED taken* 51).

59 *Burgeys*, 'burgesses', are freemen of the city, often those with some kind of civic responsibility such as magistrates (*MED burgeis* 2). *Bedels* are officers of the lawcourts or church, summoning plaintiffs and keeping order.

60 *mesters*: *MED mister*, a trade or craft.

62 *in route*: 'in a crowd'; the expression sometimes refers to a disorderly mob, *MED rout(e* n.(1) 3(e).

64 *þat as*: 'As if'.

walon: Probably from ME *wale* n. 'choice', ON *val*; see Dance 2019, 2.89–90; *Gersum* s.v. *wale*, v. Noun, verb and adjective are characteristic of alliterative poetry, in a range of senses, including 'choose, distinguish (i.e. choose between), find, perceive', though there is no parallel for the meaning 'arrived, assembled' here. Cf. *wale* l. 73. The sense-development parallels that of *chesen*, 'to choose', but used also to mean 'go, come' in alliterative verse; *MED chesen* 8.

The b-verse is formulaic: *Cleanness* 1786, and 24 instances in *DT*.

66 *sextene*: the sexton had general duties in the church, cleaning, caring for vestments and sacred ornaments, etc. So he is in charge of the sacristy where these objects were stored. The *sayntuaré*, 'sanctuary', is the area around the high altar, where the tomb is discovered.

67 After *bede*, 'ordered', infinitive *vnlouke* has passive sense, 'to be unfastened'.

68 *lome*: the same word as modern 'loom', originally an implement of any sort, as in *Gawain* 2309 denoting the Green Knight's axe, developing the sense 'container, vessel', hence in *Patience* 160 'ship', *Cleanness* 314 etc. 'the Ark', and here and in l. 149 referring to the coffin.

72 For *neuer so* with subjunctive verb in a concessive clause see *OED never* 4a, 'denoting an unlimited amount'.

73 *to wale*: lit. 'at one's choice, to choose', a common expression in alliterative verse, often, as here, no more than an intensive, 'very much'. *wale* may be construed as n. or v.; see *MED walen* 1(b).

74 *come to to know*: 'manage to understand'; no emendation is required. For *come to*, 'succeed', see *MED comen* 4a (d), citing Mannyng, *Handlyng Synne* 2672: 'he my3t neuer come to to do'.

75 *glode*: Much discussed; not the same word as modern English *glade*, though probably related. See Dance 2019, 2. 277–80 and *Gersum* s.v. *glode* for full discussions. *MED glade* n.(1) gives literary instances only from alliterative verse; in *Pearl* 79 *glodez* are the open spaces between trees through which the sun shines; in *Gawain* 2181 the grass grows 'in glodes aywhere', perhaps 'in open spaces, in patches'. Here it seems to refer to the open space of the coffin.

78–84 The body is clothed in a gown hemmed with gold-thread and pearls, buckled with a gold belt; above that is a cloak of fine material with edging of squirrel-fur; on the head is a coif under a crown, and in the hand a sceptre. The coif and the mantle lined with miniver would indicate a judge's outfit. Sir John Fortescue prescribes the appropriate dress for a judge on promotion from a sergeant of the law in 1468–71:

> Sed iusticiarius factus, loco collobii clamide induetur, firmata super humerum eius dexterum, ceteris ornamentis servientis ad huc permanentibus, excepto quod strangulata veste aut coloris departiti ut potest serviens, iusticiarius non utetur, et capicium eius non alia furrura quam menevera penulatur.

> [But having been made a justice, he shall wear in place of a cape a cloak fastened upon his right shoulder; he shall still retain the other ornaments of a serjeant, except that a judge shall not wear a striped garment or parti-coloured habit as the serjeant can, and that his robe is edged with no fur other than miniver.] (*De Laudibus Legum Anglie*, pp. 128–9.)

An inventory of goods of Sir Thomas Urswyk, chief baron of the exchequer, taken in 1479 lists among his gowns a 'skarlett clok furred with puryd menyver', and another baron of the exchequer, Sir John Holgrave (d. 1487), also owned 'a gown of scarlet purfyllyd with menyver'. See Baker 2013.

Judges often figure on memorial brasses and effigies. Some of the earliest are the brasses of Sir William de Lodyngton (d. 1419) at Gunby, Lincs, who wears a coif, a gown with a belt, and a mantle; Sir John Cassy (d. 1400) at Deerhurst, Glos, and Sir John Juyn, (d. 1439) in Bristol, both wearing coifs and gowns edged with fur; Sir Hugh de Holes (d. 1415) at Watford, Herts; and the fine stone effigy of Sir William Gascoigne (d. 1419) in All Saints Church, Harewood, Yorks. Photos of all of these are on the internet, and see Saul 2009, pp. 265-89.

88 *3orde*: 'precinct'. It was as if the clothes had been made just there and then. St Paul's churchyard was a hive of activity, deplored by Bishop Braybrooke: 'In 1385 he threatened excommunication against anyone buying or selling in the cathedral precinct, playing ball games there, or shooting at birds on the cathedral roof' (*ODNB* s.v. Braybrooke, Robert).

89 *hym þe face*: 'his face'. The dative pronoun is occasionally used to indicate possession, usually of a part of the body; e.g. 'She lighte doun and falleth hym to feet' (*CT* II.1104). See Mustanoja 1960, pp. 98-9.

92 *in sounde*: 'in good health'; cf. *Gawain* 2489, 'kny3t al in sounde'.

93 *space*: 'time', its original sense, as again at l. 312. Cf. Chaucer, *Parliament of Fowls* 67: 'in certeyn yeres space'.

95-100 The excited onlookers are confused and voice conflicting opinions. How long has he been lying there? Some say the unspoilt state of the body and clothes shows that the burial was recent. Yet the body of someone of such importance would have been long remembered, and indeed the crown and sceptre suggest he must have been a king. Yet the depth of the burial indicates that it is ancient. And some say it's remarkable that no one has reported seeing him.

101 *note*: Wrongly glossed 'designation, name' by *MED note* n.(3), 5(b). Rather it is 'business, effort' (*MED note* n.(2), 3(a)). Cf. 38n and 152n.

nourne: The verb is found elsewhere only in *Gawain* and *Cleanness*, with a basic sense 'declare, speak'. For discussion of its origins see Dance 2019, 2.81. See also ll. 152, 195.

102 No evidence can be found wherever they search. A *title* is something written, such as an inscription, a book or part of a book. See l. 28 for a legal application. A *token* is physical evidence, such as a coin or a ring, while a *tale* is an oral report.

103 *breuyt*: the primary sense is 'write', *MED breven* 1; Dance 2019, 2.196–7. The sense 'declare, speak of' is recorded in *Gawain* 465, 1393, 1488, and frequently in the *Wars*; *MED breven* 3. It contrasts here with *notyd*.

104 *more ne lasse*: for the sense 'at all' see *MED mor(e* adv. 1 (i).

105 Cf. 'And bodword to þe bischop broȝt of his come' (*Wars* 1581).

108 *Sir Erkenwolde*: 'Sir' is used of priests as well as knights; cf. 'thou preest, com hyder thou, sir John' (*CT* VII.2810).

an abbay: Bede (iv.6) reports that Erkenwald founded two abbeys, his own at Chertsey in Surrey and another at Barking in Essex for his sister Ethelburga as first abbess. Barking is ten miles from St Paul's.

to visite: that is, to conduct an episcopal inspection; *MED visiten* 2(b).

113 *By þat*: 'when'.

114 *meere*: 'landmark, place', referring to St Paul's; for the same sense see *Wars* 5184. Originally 'boundary' (*MED mere* n.(3)).

115–16 Instead of rushing to inspect the body ('þe dede') Erkenwald retires to the bishop's palace and spends the night in prayer. Of the palace in 1603 Stow writes: 'On the north west side of this Church yeard is the Bishops pallace, a large thing for receipt, wherein divers kinges have been lodged, and great housholde hath beene kept, as appeareth by the great Hall' (Stow 1908, 2.20).

117 *day-belle*: *MED dai* 13(a) quotes *Havelok* 1132: 'On the morwen, hwan day was sprungen, And day-belle at kirke rungen'. For this line and variations upon it see Turville-Petre 1977, 86.

119 *naytyd* (MS *nattyd*): The usual expression is 'say his hours', i.e. recite the prayers allotted to the canonical hours. With the sense here cf. perhaps *Gawain* 65: 'Nowel nayted onewe, neuened ful ofte', 'Christmas called out once again, often named'. The verb *naiten* is rare outside alliterative verse, its basic sense being 'use'. See *Gersum*, s.v. *nayte*.

123 *digne*: 'condescend to grant' (*MED deinen*). Erkenwald prays that this mystery may strengthen the faith of his flock. Cf. l. 175. The shift to *þi* (124) from *his* marks the direct address to God.

128 *matens*: the early morning prayers.

130 *prestly*: 'promptly', with a pun on 'as a priest' (*MED prestli* adv.(2)).

131-2 The mass of *Spiritus Domini* is a votive mass for the Holy Spirit, beginning 'Spiritus domini replevit orbem terrarum' – 'The spirit of the Lord fills the whole earth' (*Sarum Missal*, ed. Legg, p. 385). The Gospel reading is John 14. 23-31, including 'the Paraclete, the Holy Ghost, whom the Father will send in my name, he will teach you all things' (John 14.26). A votive mass is for use on special occasions, as here where the Holy Spirit has granted Erkenwald 'an ansuare' (127) and the bishop celebrates mass 'for his spede', for success. See Whatley 1982, 278-9 and n. 10, rejecting earlier suggestions that the reference is to the mass of Pentecost.

133 *questis*: 'sounds'. The usual senses of *quest* are 'enquiry, search', hence 'search for game, hunt'. In a transferred sense it refers to the baying of hunting dogs, as in *Gawain* 1150, 'þe fyrst quethe of þe quest'. Here the 'queme questis' are not dogs but the lovely voices of the choir. For the same surprising comparison see Gace, *Le Roman de Deduis*, cited and translated by Putter 2006, 376-9: 'There is no response or alleluia that was ever sung in the royal chapel, however fine and beautiful, that ever gave so much pleasure as it does to hear such a hunt. Some hounds sing a *motet*, others a *double hocket*, the biggest sing the tenor, others the countertenor.'

135 For the meanings and restricted distribution of *reken* see Borroff 1962, pp. 98-9.

136 *later ende*: 'latter part'; cf. *St Editha*, ed. Horstmann, 2219-20: 'Bot in the laterhende of þe office sodenliche / Seynt Ede apperede hem bodylyche to'.

137-42 Erkenwald and his entourage walk from the chancel across the paved floor to a locked enclosure in the sanctuary where the body lies. Cf. l. 66. The *cloyster* refers to an 'enclosed area', as in *Gawain* 804, where Gawain hopes to see the enclosure within the castle.

138 *plied*: 'bowed' (*MED plien* v.(1) 1(b)).

141 *pyne*: 'discomfort' or 'difficulty' because of the large crowd following Erkenwald. Cf. *Patience* 91; *Gawain* 123.

144 The dean is in charge of the cathedral and second only to the bishop.

145 Cf. *Wars* 1213, 'hym myntis with his fyngir'.

152 *note*: Both *OED* and *MED* take this to mean 'fame, repute' (*MED note* n.(3), 3(b)), and it is true this has possible support from *Cleanness* 1651, 'So watz noted þe note of Nabugodenozar' (where *note* probably means 'fame', but possibly 'action'). But more meaningful in context is *MED note* n.(2), 2(b), 'occupation', quoting the gloss 'dede of occupacyon, opus, occupacio', and cf. *CT* I.4068 where the miller 'dooth his note' – goes about his business.

nourne of one speche: 'state a single word, say anything at all'. Cf. 101n.

153–6 The dean and his staff are puzzled at the complete lack of any record, since the deaths of much poorer people have been recorded in the cathedral's *martilage*, the register of those who have been buried there. The cathedral library had an extensive collection, but most of the manuscripts that survived the Middle Ages perished in 1666 in the Great Fire of London. See Ker 1964, 120, and 1969, 240–62.

154 *þat ... his*: 'Whose'.

157 *to loke hit by kynde*: 'to observe it in terms of natural signs', i.e. the physical condition of the body.

159–76 For analysis of Erkenwald's speech see Introduction, pp. 49–51.

161 *Toward*: 'In relation to, in comparison with'.

165 *lettes ... litell*: 'it hinders him very little', i.e. it causes little difficulty to God.

167 *þereas*: '(In the situation) where'.

oute swarues: 'swerves away (i.e. deviates/departs) from'.

170 *at oureselfe*: 'from among ourselves'.

171 *glow*: related to the noun *glee*, so 'entertain, make merry'. The sense here, 'call out' is otherwise recorded only in *Patience* 164: 'vchon glewed on his god', translating 'clamaverunt'.

173 *fastynge*: 'confirming, strengthening'.

174 *vertues*: 'powers'; the primary sense.

176 *talent*: 'desire, wish', a sense adopted from French.

frende: cf. *Pearl* 1204: 'A God, a Lorde, a frende ful fyin'.

177 This line begins with an enlarged capital, at the exact mid-point of the poem.

179 *þou* (1): The scribe writes *þᵘ*, which makes sense but is perhaps a mistake for *þ⁹* (*þus*) or *þ'* (*þer*).

181 Cf. *Wars* 534: 'he was boune at hire bode'.

183 The living must 'believe' what the dead 'know for certain'.

187 *lagh*: 'religious law, religion', MED *laue* 4a.

190 *brayed*: MED *breiden* v.(1) has a range of senses, including 'move, twist, turn', as in *Gawain* 440, and 'wake up'. Here 'stirred, roused from sleep' would be appropriate.

191 *dreme*: This is MED *drem* n.(1), 'sound, voice'.

192 The line gives a deliberately enigmatic explanation of how the dead body came to speak. It is the 'graunte ... of the Holy Goste' (126–7), just as the Holy Spirit descended upon the people at Pentecost 'and they began to speak with divers tongues, according as the Holy Ghost gave them to speak' (Acts 2.4). Separated from its soul, which is in limbo, the body is unquestionably dead (116, 225, 309), but here is granted a 'a sort of spirit-life' enabling it to speak. This should be interpreted in the light of l. 272, where the body says that God 'has lant me to last', and l. 315, where Erkenwald says to the body 'Oure Lord lene ... þat þou lyfe hades'. In each case God grants the dead body life so that it may be baptised. MED *lenen* v.(3) is 'to give, grant, bestow', often with an implication that the gift is temporary, as here. The primary meaning of *goste* at this date is, as glossed by OED *ghost* 1, 'an animating or vital principle' (OED sense 14, 'a faint appearance or insubstantial semblance', is post-medieval), and *goste-lyfe* may be understood as a compound, 'spirit-life'. Compare *Cleanness* 325, where God vows to destroy all living creatures, 'Alle þat glydez and gotz and gost of lyf habbez', where *goste of lyfe* means 'animating spirit (i.e. breath) of life', translating Genesis 6.17, 'spiritus vitae'. Quinn 1984a discusses the theological issues, citing Aquinas. On the presence of the Holy Spirit throughout the poem, see Borroff 2006b.

In the b-verse *al* has been emended to *lyfe* to supply alliteration.

194 *for bothe myn eghen*: literally 'at the cost of both my eyes', i.e. 'upon pain of my life', an expression found elsewhere, particularly in alliterative verse. Cf. *Wynnere* 126, *Wars* 1908, 5169.

195 *nournet me after*: 'addressed me by'; cf. l. 101n. Erkenwald has commanded the body in the name of Jesus, ll. 180–1, and the judge now makes this statement of recognition of Christ as God almighty.

198 *One þe vnhapnest*: 'The most unfortunate'. For the construction in which *one* strengthens a superlative, compare *Gawain* 137 'On þe moste' 'the very most', 2363 'on þe fautlest', 'the most faultless'.

199 *kyng ... cayser ... kny3t*: A traditional collocation; cf. *Wynnere* 327, *Piers Plowman* C.22.101, etc.

200 *vsit*: 'occupied, dwelt in'; MED *usen* 10(b), OED *use* v. 18a.

202 *sayd causes*: 'legal actions brought'; MED *seien* v.(1), 2b(g); *cause* 7.

205 *lewid*: For the usual senses see MED *leued* and OED *lewd*. They include 'ignorant', 'uneducated', 'stupid', 'useless', 'evil', none of which is appropriate for a *date*, 'period of time'. Following previous editors, MED *leued* 1(f) suggests '?unknown, ?forgotten', but the judge goes on to give precise if riddling calculations. Possibly the phrase means 'a horribly long time'.

206–10 Many have attempted to work out the 'lewid date', but it has indeed proved 'too much for anyone to make a number of'. Is it a deliberate puzzle? The form of the calculations would have been familiar. According to the mid-fifteenth-century transcript in BL MS Harley 565, a large tablet hung in St Paul's by the tomb of Bishop Roger Niger. Its text began 'In principio creauit deus celum et terram' ('In the beginning God created heaven and earth'), and, after detailing the length of five Ages, continued 'The years from the beginning of the world to the incarnation of our Lord Jesus Christ: 5099. The years from his incarnation to his Passion: 33 years, not completed. The years from the creation of the world to the building of Troy: 4030 years. From the destruction of Troy to the building of New Troy, which is now called London: 64 years. From the building of New Troy up to the building of the city of Rome: 380 years. From the founding of the city to the coming of Christ: 715 years. From the beginning of the world 4084 years after the destruction of Troy, thus 1150 years before the birth of Christ' (BL MS Harley 565, ff. 4r–5r, my translation). The account continues with Brutus landing in Britain and founding New Troy during the reign of Eli and the capture of the Ark of the Covenant, and proceeds with a potted history of kings to Henry VI in 1431. It can be observed that computing the dates of events requires a good deal of adding and subtracting, and even so the figures do not seem entirely correct. Similar 'historical' tablets hung in York and other cathedrals; see Kerby-Fulton 2021, pp. 268–78.

The judge says *either* that he was buried 482 (500 – 18) years after London was founded by Brutus and 1054 (1000 + 30 + [3 × 8]) years before the birth of Christ, *or* (as punctuated here) 482 BC and 1054 years before the discovery of his body. Neither can be quite accurate, and the lack of alliteration in 208 is suspicious. Geoffrey of Monmouth says that Brutus built New Troy when 'the priest Eli was ruling in Judea and the Ark of the Covenant was captured by the Philistines' (i.18), taking this from Nennius, *Historia Brittonum*. According to Isidore, *Etymologiae* chap. 5, xxxix.12, the date of the capture of the Ark was near the end of the third age, 4084 years after Creation, and therefore 1126 BC (cf. the tablet above). Robert Mannyng is not far off this dating, saying that 'Þe tyme Brutus aryued here / A thousand and tuo hundreth 3ere / So mykelle was it þer beforn / Are Ihesu was of Mary born' (*Chronicle* 1745-8). We learn from the poem that the judge lived in the reign of Belinus (l. 213), who, according to Geoffrey, invaded Rome. Livy, *Ab urbe condita* 5.35-55, gives the date of the sack of Rome as 390 BC. Emending *fife* to *foure* would give 382 BC (400 - 18) as the date of the burial, and 672 AD (1054 - 382) as the date of the discovery, not quite within Erkenwald's episcopate (675-93). The important point is that the judge was a pagan living long before the birth of Christ.

211 *heire of anoye*: 'inheritor of suffering', i.e. the reverse of 'eyres of heuene' (*Piers Plowman* C.5.59). See *MED heir* 1(e), quoting Audelay, 'Into herþ he [Christ] come / To make þer eyrus of heuen blys'. Living before Christ, the judge has not been entitled to the inheritance of heavenly bliss but is one of the 'children of wrath' (Ephesians 2.3) that Paul says are not saved through Christ. Elsewhere Paul writes: 'We are the sons of God. And if sons, heirs also; heirs indeed of God and joint heirs with Christ' (Romans 8.16-17).

213-16 Belinus, king of Britain, quarrelled with his brother Brennius, but eventually they were reconciled and set out together to conquer Rome (Geoffrey iii.1-10). Belinus was a great builder (Billingsgate was supposedly named after him) and he 'ratified the laws which his father had drawn up. He proclaimed that justice should be administered fairly throughout his kingdom' (Geoffrey iii.5). These were the so-called Molmutine Laws. Later Arthur refers to Belinus as 'that most glorious of the kings of the Britons' (Geoffrey ix.16). To be chief judge during the reign of the justest of kings was to represent the summit of *gentile lawe*, 'pagan justice'.

214 *Bitter* (ms. *Mony one*): the alliteration fails.

217-18 The silence of the observers is in dramatic contrast to their previous hubbub.

224 How is it, asks Erkenwald, that you wear a crown and hold a sceptre, since you were never a king holding land bound by feudal tenure, nor had royal powers over the lives of subjects? A liege man owed allegiance and feudal duties to his lord or king in return for his land holding. A poem on the duties and powers of Henry V states that 'Eche a kyng haþ Goddis powere / Of lyf and leme to saue and spille' (*Digby Poems* 12.105–06).

226 To dispel any imputation of arrogance, the judge makes it clear that he did not ask to be arrayed in this way.

227 *MED* records only this instance of *deputate* as a noun, but cf. *MED depute* n., quoting Reginald Pecock: the prince shall 'ordeyne vndir hym deputees or officers, mynistris to execute hise lawis'.

229 *on gentile wise*: The judge says that he did as well as a pagan possibly could, as in l. 242. The same expression is used in *Cleanness* 1432, describing the actions of Nebuchadnezzar. In both cases there is perhaps a pun on *gentile*, 'gentile' and 'noble', just as Jonah is 'jentyle prophete', both noble prophet and prophet to the gentiles (*Patience* 62).

230 *faithe* is 'a loaded word' (Whatley 1986, 349) in relation to the judge, rewarded for his faithfulness to principles of justice and rectitude, 'þe fynest of faith' (252) in the eyes of contemporaries, yet *faitheles* (287) in Christian terms, and therefore unrewarded.

232 The first mention of *riȝte*, 'justice, what is right', which becomes a leading theme.

233–44 These lines reflect the oath taken by judges and others in positions of authority, as recorded in variant versions, in Latin, French and English, in which a judge swore to administer justice without fear or favour. Building on Deuteronomy 16.18–19, the future Pope Innocent III described God's justice:

> Ipse est iudex iustus, fortis et longanimis, qui nec prece, nec precio, nec amore nec odio declinat a semita rectitudinis, set via recta semper incedens, nullum malum preterit impunitum, nullum bonum irremuneratum relinquit. (*De miseria conditionis humane*, ed. Lewis, 3.14)

> [He is the just judge, strong and patient, who neither for supplication nor for reward, nor love nor hate, turns aside from the

path of justice but, always proceeding on the right road, he leaves no evil unpunished and no good unrewarded.]

This is expanded in the oath prescribed for appointments to the King's Council in 1257:

> Item, quod libere permittent de seipsis, amicis, et consanguineis justitiam fieri cuicumque petenti. Nec per eos impedietur justicia fieri prece vel pretio, favore vel odio, sed bona fide procurabunt, quod magnus sicut parvus judicetur, secundum legem et consuetudinem regni. Nec sustentabunt vel defendent injuriantes in injuriis suis, opere vel sermone. (*Annales monastici*, 1.395–6)

> [Item, that they shall allow justice to be freely done to anyone seeking it against themselves, their friends and their relatives. And justice shall not be impeded by them for request nor for reward, for favour nor for hatred, but they shall in good faith arrange that great as well as small be judged according to the law and the custom of the realm. And they shall not support or defend those who do harm and the harm they do by deed or by word.]

In 1258 this was further expanded in Anglo-Norman for Edward I's justices in eyre in the Close Roll for 1277–8, part of which reads:

> Dreiture a vostre poer freez a tuz ausibien as povres com as riches, e qe pur hautesce ne pur richeyce, ne pur hayne ne pur favur, ne pur poer ne pur estat de nuli persone, ne pur bienfet, doun, ne promesse de nulli qe fet vus soit ou vus purra estre fet, ne par art ne par engyn, autri dreiture ne desturberez ne respiterez cuntre resun ne cuntre les leis de la terre; mes saunz regard de nul istat ne de persone leaument freez fere dreiture a chescun solum les leys usees. (TNA C 54/95)

> [As far as you are able you will do justice to all, to poor as to rich, and neither for high status nor for wealth, nor for hatred nor for favour, nor for power or rank of anyone, nor for benefit, gift or promise of anyone which is made to you or could be made to you, nor by trickery nor by device, you will not prevent or delay justice against right nor against the laws of the land;

but without regard for status or for person you will loyally have justice done to everyone according to the laws in use.]

The catalogue of lines 233-4 matches the Latin *vel ... vel* and the French *ne pur ... ne pur*, as do the motives of *wrathe* (*odio*, *hayne*) and *mede* (*pretio*, *doun*). The malign influence of the powerful expressed in lines 234 and 239-40 reflects the French 'pur hautesce ne pur richeyce' and 'pur poer ne pur estat'. The tricks and deceits of l. 238 are the *art* and *engyn* of the French, echoed by *gynful* in the poem. That a judge must not be swayed by filial affection (243-4) is the point of the Latin command to exercise justice towards *consanguineis*. See Burrow 2004; Turville-Petre 2008. On the forms of the oaths, see Brand 2001.

235 *by reson myn awen*: 'according to my own judgement', which is necessarily limited by his paganism. Cf. l. 242.

237 *Declynet*: in Deuteronomy 16.19 the judges must not 'in alterem partem declinent' – 'go aside to either part'; Proverbs 4.27 has 'Ne declines ad dexteram neque ad sinistram' – 'Decline not to the right hand nor to the left'. Cf. *De miseria* above.

240 *meschefe*, in general 'trouble, difficulty', may refer to the 'wickedness' of those menacing a judge (*monnes manas*), or to the 'poverty' of those for whom a judge might feel *routhe*; see MED *mischef* 1(a), 4 and 2 respectively.

241 *þe hegh gate*: 'the true path', translating 'semita rectitudinis'; the expression is also in *Pearl* 395, where the Maiden's good fortune is 'the main avenue' of the Dreamer's happiness.

242 His conscience, informed only by his pagan faith, had limited understanding of the true path.

243-4 In the two subordinate clauses governed by *þagh* the subject pronoun is omitted, heightening the rhetorical chiasmus. See Mustanoja 1960, pp. 141-3.

247 *morte* (ms. *dethe*): The emendation corrects the alliteration. Cf. *Wars* 1402: 'Þe morth [D ms. morte] of all þe Messedones'.

248 *to bounty*: 'in my honour'.

249 Cf. *court haldes*, 'presides over the court' (*Gawain* 53).

250-2 The judge explains the symbolism of his mantle, girdle of gold, and miniver.

255 *schulde*: 'would be'. After an auxiliary verb the infinitive may be understood from a previous form of the verb (here *wos*). Cf. *Gawain* 1544: 'As I am, oþer euer schal'.

257 *baythes*: 'asks, questions'; elsewhere the word is only recorded three times in *Gawain* in the sense 'agree, consent'. From ON *beiða*, 'ask for'; see *Gersum* s.v. *bayþe*.

262 The line has caused difficulty. For *thar*, 'may', see *MED thurven*, which has a wide range of senses, expressing necessity, obligation and, here, possibility, *MED* sense 7a(a). The ms. reading may be *ryue*, 'tear' or more probably *ryne*, 'touch, pierce', and *rote* might be verb or noun, here understood as noun, emending 'ne rote' to 'no rote'.

263 The *coloure* refers to the judge's clothing, as in 148.

264 *monnes lore* is parallel to *monnes counsell* (266), denoting human skills limited in comparison to the powers of the king of reason (267).

267 *kyng of reson*: here *reson* refers to the fundamental principle of justice, the *ratio divina*. See *MED resoun* n.(2) 3(a); and cf. 'contre resoun' in the Anglo-Norman oath above. The sense is common in *Piers Plowman*; see Alford 1988a, p. 134, and Alford 1988b.

alowes: 'gives credit for', hence 'rewards'. The context shows that it has something of its legal sense, 'to admit something as valid and legitimate', suggested by *lawes* in the next line and the judge's repetition of *riȝt* (267, 269, 271–2). God, king of justice, rewards justice above all merits. See Alford 1988a, p. 4; and Whatley 1984b, 2–5, who compares the usage in *Piers Plowman* B.12.310, 'Ne wolde neuere trewe god but trewe treuth were allowed', on the subject of Trajan's salvation for his *truþe*. See next note.

268 Langland offers the best guide to the scope of *trouthe* in relation to God in Holychurch's sermon, *Piers Plowman* C.1.81–202, beginning and ending 'When alle tresores ben tried, Treuthe is the beste'. Contextually, the emphasis is upon just actions and, more generally, doing what is right.

269–72 On the artful positioning of *riȝt* in this passage see Putter et al. 2007, pp. 161–2.

272 *lant me to last*: cf. l. 192.

273 *sayes þou*: 'what do you say'. It might be emended to imp. sg. *say*.

274 *stablid*: 'established, located', *MED stablen* v.(1) cites this under sense 7(a) 'ground (the soul) morally', but the bishop asks in what district of

heaven the judge's soul is placed. The sense is reinforced by collocation with *stadde*, 'fixed'. Cf. *Gawain* 33, 'stad and stoken'.

275 Compare 'Judge me, O Lord, according to my justice' (Psalm 7.9).

276 It is apparent from lines 279–80 that Erkenwald assumes God has rewarded the judge for his devotion to justice.

278 The bishop's belief on who will be saved is based on two very similar psalms: 'Lord, who shall dwell in thy tabernacle? Or who shall rest in thy holy hill? He that walketh without blemish [sine macula] and worketh justice [operatur justitiam]' (Psalm 14.1–2), and 'Who shall ascend into the mountain of the Lord, or who shall stand in his holy place? The innocent in hands [innocens manibus] and clean of heart [mundo corde]' (Psalm 23.3–4). The maiden in *Pearl*, discussing the heavenly rewards for the just and the innocent, cites the same psalms, and identifies 'þe ry3twys man' and 'þe harmlez haþel' (675–6). So the *skilfulle* is 'þe ry3twys man' who 'worketh justice'; cf. *Pearl* in the same section: 'Two men to saue is God by skylle' (674), i.e. God will justly save two men. The *vnskathely* (cf. *scathe*, 'harm') is 'þe harmlez haþel' who is 'innocent' and 'without blemish'. 'The fact that versions of Psalms 14 or 23 appear at key moments in *Piers Plowman* B, *St Erkenwald* and *Pearl* suggests that Middle English poetry persistently returns to thematic issues of law, "meed" and merit. These psalms frequently produce interest in the related ideas of human and divine justice and reward, legal ethics and salvific decision making' (Jones 2017, p. 234).

skelton: 'hasten'? *Gersum*, s.v. *scelt*, proposes an ON origin *skella*, noting that 'the apparent range of senses in context is varied and contested'. The verb appears only here and four times in various senses in *Cleanness*; cf. 'Scoleres skelten þeratte þe skyl for to fynde' (1554) of attempts to interpret the writing on the wall, where 'hurried' is a possible meaning. In *DT* the phrase 'skeltyng of harme' is used twice (1089, 6042), with a possible sense of 'approach of danger'. However, Breeze 2009, 147–8, proposes an Irish etymology.

280 *restorment*: Alluding to Acts 3.21, 'the times of the restitution [restitutionis] of all things'.

285 *vnpreste*: 'not prepared', because he has not been baptised. *MED unpreste* follows earlier editors with the inappropriate gloss 'ignorant', but the primary sense of *preste* is 'ready, prepared'.

plite: God's covenant with man, renewed by Christ; *MED plight* 1(d). See Hebrews 8.6–13.

283–4 Note the alliterative play on *maȝty/myghtes/myȝt*, modified by *mercy* (284 and 286).

291 The Harrowing of Hell is described in the apocryphal Gospel of Nicodemus (fourth century). Between his Crucifixion and Resurrection, Christ released the souls of the righteous, including Adam, from the *limbus patrum*, the 'limbo of the fathers'. Versions of the story were widespread, as in the *Legenda aurea* and the mystery plays. Langland gives a memorable account in *Piers Plowman* C.22. For the theology, see Introduction pp. 27–35.

292 *loffynge*: MED *loffinge* glosses 'remnant', citing this one instance. If this is right, it refers to Romans 9.27 (in which Paul quotes Isaiah 10.22): 'If the number of the children of Israel be as the sand of the sea, a remnant [reliquiae] shall be saved'; and cf. Romans 11.5: 'there is a remnant saved according to the election of grace'. The related noun is MED *love* n.(2), 'remainder', citing *The Life of St Cuthbert* 1306: 'Half his brede his horse he gaue / And kepit to himself þe laue'.

294 Hugh Ripelin categorises the four regions of hell – the hell of the damned, purgatory, the limbo of infants and the limbo of the fathers – in terms of their 'sensible pain [pena sensus]', 'pain of loss [pena dampni et non sensus]' and interior or exterior darkness. In the limbo of the fathers 'there was the pain of loss and not sensible pain, and there was exterior darkness but not a loss of grace. Christ descended to this place and rescued his people from there' (*Compendium Theologicae veritatis*, p. 198). This categorisation is based on Aquinas, *Commentary on the Sentences* III, d. 22., q. 2, a. 1, qcla. 2. Introduction pp. 31–2, and Turville-Petre 2023a.

295–9 The judge states the doctrine of atonement, central to the poem, in which original sin which condemned mankind is redeemed through the Crucifixion and remitted through baptism. The doctrine was developed by St Paul: e.g. 'Wherefore as by one man (Adam) sin entered into this world and by sin death, and so death passed upon all men' (Romans 5.12); and 'As in Adam all die, so also in Christ all shall be made alive' (1 Corinthians 15.22).

296 *plyȝtles*: the primary meaning is 'without guilt', i.e. free of actual sin but condemned by orginal sin, 'Adam's plight' (*MED plight* 1(c)). There is perhaps a pun on 'without a covenant'; cf. *plite* (285), a sense probably influenced by the verb *plighten*, 'pledge'.

poysned: In *Cleanness* also the fatal apple poisoned Adam and his descendants: 'þurȝ þe eggyng of Eue he ete of an apple / Þat enpoysned alle peplez þat parted fro hem boþe' (241–2). So too in *Death and Liffe* 272–3. For the theology see Romans 5.12–17. Here the poison requires the *medecyn* of baptism.

297 *tethe*: A striking image. Adam's teeth became poisonous by biting into the apple. Other editors make the easy emendation to the less vivid reading *teche*, 'sin'.

take in: either 'swallow, consume', with *take* as present, or 'caught up in', with the verb as past participle, parallel to *entouchid* (*MED taken* 12(a) and 2a(b)). The former is more consistent with the imagery of poison and medicine. Emendation to past tense *toke(n)* is a possibility, though the cleansing of original sin continues to require baptism.

glotte: 'filth, slime', figuratively 'sin, corruption'. As a medical term it refers to mucus within the body, so in *Patience* 269 Jonah passes through *glette* into the stomach of the whale. In *Cleanness* 573 the filthy *glette* of Sodom brings about its destruction. See *Gersum* s.v. *glotte* for discussion of its form, which should perhaps be emended to *glette*.

299 Langland's Good Samaritan has the same spiritual *medicyne* for the injuries of the man who falls among thieves: baptism followed by penance and the Eucharist (*Piers Plowman* C.19.83–95).

301 *wele dede*, 'good works', are insufficient without *faitheful bileue*. 'If Abraham were justified by works, he hath whereof to glory, but not before God' (Romans 4.2). See also Ephesians 2.8–9.

302 *depe lake*: the phrase is from the offertory of the mass for the dead: 'Libera animas omnium fidelium defunctorum de poenis inferni et de profundo lacu': 'Deliver the souls of all the faithful departed from the pains of hell and from the deep pit' (*Sarum Missal*, p. 433). For this sense of *lake* see *MED lak(e* n. 1, 3(c), citing 'Maiden & Moder Cum & Se' where Christ says he will rescue souls 'in helle lake' (Brown 1957, pp. 85–6).

303 *þat soper*: the eschatological feast, the 'marriage supper of the Lamb' (Revelation 19.9), which Christ had announced at the Last Supper: 'You may eat and drink at my table in my kingdom' (Luke 22.30).

304 The judge appropriately alludes to Matthew 5.6: 'Blessed are they that hunger and thirst after justice, for they shall have their fill.'

306 *dymly* is both 'in the gloom' and 'abjectly'; cf. *Patience* 375, 'dymly biso3ten'. In the *Commedia* Virgil, who is in limbo as a preChristian, 'Non per far, ma per non fare' ('not for doing but for not doing'), describes it to Dante: 'Luogo è là giù non tristo da martìri, / ma di

tenebre solo, ove i lamenti / non suonan come guai, ma son sospiri' ('There is a place below, sad not with torments but only with darkness, where the laments have no sound of wailing but are sighs') (*Purgatorio* 7.28–30). The line echoes line 294.

307 *herken after*: contextually perhaps 'look out for': compare Mirk's *Festial*, 52.20–1, where St Laurence 'herkenud ȝarne aftur þore men and wommen and ȝode to hem and ȝaf to hem þat neded mete and drink and cloþus'.

308 *ho*: 'she' (the judge's soul), who has long waited for an invitation to the supper.

311–2 Erkenwald had raised his eyes in line 178 as he began speaking, and now he lowers them in sorrow, weeping so copiously he had no *space*, 'time, opportunity', to speak. His tears are *lauande*, 'flowing freely' but also 'washing' clean of sin; see *MED laven*; Whatley 1986, 352. On the subject of penitential laundering Langand (*Piers Plowman* C.16.335a) quotes Psalm 50.9: 'Lavabis me, et super nivem dealbabor', 'Thou shalt wash me and I shall be made whiter than snow.'

315–19 All the requirements of the sacrament are met in this inadvertent baptism, as they are set out in *The Lay Folks' Catechism*, a guide to basic Christian belief:

> To this sacrement falles foure thinges,
> If it sal rightly be taken as Hali Kirk techis:
> Ane is right saying and shap of the wordes
> That him augh for to sai that gyffes this sacrement,
> That er thise: 'I baptise the in the name
> Of the Fadir and the Son and the Hali Gast.
> Another is that it be done anely in water,
> For nan othir licour is leueful tharfore.
> The third is that he that gyffes this sacrement
> Be in wit and in will for to gyff it.
> And the ferthe is that he that takes it
> Be nouther of lered ne of lawed baptised before. (282–93)

For the standard instructions and discussion see Aquinas, *Summa Theologiae* 3, q. 66.

319 *not one grue lenger*: Quinn 1984b interprets this as 'and nothing more', i.e. with no additional words that would invalidate the baptism,

but the construction is 'for long enough (316) ... and not a moment longer'. Erkenwald is asking for just a small miracle rather than the resuscitation of the body. For *grue* cf. *Gawain* 2251, 'I shal gruch þe no grwe', 'I won't harbour the slightest ill-will'.

320 *daungerde*: The usual senses of *(en)daungeren* are 'to render (legally) liable, to bring into debt'. Perhaps Erkenwald is saying that, provided the judge died *after* he had been baptised, he would (as it were) have no claim against the bishop for not doing his duty by him.

321 The collocation *werpen wordes*, 'speak' (repeated in 329), is common in alliterative verse: cf. *Cleanness* 213: 'With þis worde þat he warp'.

324 *sadde*: 'reverent'. Previously the judge had spoken *gronyng* (282) and *dulfully* (309). Now, having joined the Christian community, he speaks of *Oure Sauyoure* and *vs* (333), whereas previously he had referred to *ȝour Criste* (209).

louyd: 'praised' (*MED loven* v.(2)). So also *louynge* (349).

330 *bourne*: literally 'river', recalling the baptism of Christ in the River Jordan. Analysed by Burrow 1997, 127.

334 The flash of light in the dark abyss is the central feature of the Chester play 'Harrowing of Hell', where Esayus (Isaiah) says:

> Yea, secerlye, this ilke light
> Comys from Goddes Sonne almight,
> For so I prophecyed aright
> Whyle that I was livinge. (17.25–8)

The reference is to Isaiah 9.2: 'The people that walked in darkness have seen a great light'.

336 *cenacle*: 'dining-room'. The Last Supper is held in 'coenaculum magnum', where Christ promises his apostles 'that you may eat and drink at my table, in my kingdom' (Luke 22.12, 30).

337 *marciall*: the 'marshall of the hall' was in charge of protocol, including seating arrangements etc. At the wedding feast in *Cleanness* the guests 'ful manerly with marchal' were 'made for to sitte' (91). Here he finds the judge's soul a *rowme*, 'place' (not 'room').

345 *sesyd in*: a legal expression, 'put in possession of'. The same phrase in the same context is used in *Pearl* 417, where the maiden is 'sesed in alle hys herytage' – put in possession of all Christ's inheritance of

heaven. Now the judge too has a right to the inheritance of eternal life promised by St Paul (Romans 8.17–18).

346 *crafte*: i.e. the human body as part of the physical world crafted by God as opposed to the *soule*. A rather odd usage, though for the great range of senses see *OED craft* n. Closest to the sense here is *Patience* 131, where God summons the storm that was part of his created world: 'He calde on þat ilk crafte he carf with his hondes'.

347–8 In the light of everlasting life, the vanity of the body, so prized on earth, is of no value. 'Vanity of vanities, and all is vanity' (Ecclesiastes 1.2). The body, described so lovingly in lines 73–92, is now a *vayneglorie*.

351 The people, earlier divided and troublesome, are now united in their celebratory procession.

352 The miraculous ringing of bells to celebrate a joyous event is found elsewhere, as in Chaucer's *Troilus and Criseyde* 3.188–9, where Pandarus claims to hear bells ring 'withouten hond' celebrating Criseyde's acceptance of Troilus. In saints' lives the miracle is taken as proof of sanctity: when the tomb of St Ethedreda is uncovered, her body is 'withouȝt ony corrupcione of hurre fleysshe', the sick are miraculously cured 'and also bellus rongen and maden gret noy / Withouȝt ony touchyng of monnes honde' (*St Etheldreda* 840, 824–5). For further examples see Tatlock 1914 and Barry 1915.

Appendix: The Glosses

Throughout the manuscript a hand of perhaps the late sixteenth century has underlined obsolete words and provided marginal glosses in the English texts. If this glosser could not interpret a word, he commonly marked it with '∴' in the margin, occasionally returning when a gloss occurred to him. Below are listed the glosses for the vocabulary of *St Erkenwald*.

Words underlined	Marginal Gloss
25 hatte	was called
29 dryghtyn	Ld master
37 buggyd	builded
46 ferly	wonderful
47 thryuandly	artificialy e.... *written over* ∴
48 gargeles	ςάμένγς *followed by* ∴
49 sperl	*illegible*
50 menskefully	∴
52 roynyshe	∴
61 lepen	ran
62 radly	
68 lengyd	
69 wy3t	skilful
73 wehes	∴
88 3epely	(finely) skilfully

Words underlined	Marginal Gloss
93 spyr	aske
95 lere	cheeke
96 weghe	∴
98 kith	∴
99 derfe	∴
100 segge	∴
116 ditte	shutte
118 vghten	∴
119 nattyd	∴
124 fulsen	help: fylstan, [in mock Caroline minuscule] in-....
127 dawid	it was day
139 rayked	went
142 burynes	grave, throw
146 lyche	body
149 lome	..vas ∴
158 malte	∴
161 weldes	possesses
163 matyd	(frustrated)
164 redeles	unprofitable, without counsel
171 glow	looke
179 lykhame	body
182 bende	∴
186 weghe	∴
189 segge	
190 brayed	∴
192 lant	∴
198 hathel	∴

Appendix: The Glosses

Words underlined	Marginal Gloss
200 lagh	∴
203 parage	parentage
207 buggid	builded
209 kynned	was borne
211 anoye	∴
214 busmare	reproach
216 enioynyd	∴
220 forwrast	∴
233 wothe	∴
238 gynful	∴
241 glent	∴
245 reken	∴
250 monlokest	
251 gurden	∴
251 graythist	∴
254 kene	stoute
258 worthe	be, com to pas
260 rattes	∴
269 menskes	honours
271 renkes	∴
278 skelton	∴
287 freke	∴
291 herghdes	∴
296 ply3tles	∴
297 glotte	∴
308 segge	∴
308 lathe	invite

Words underlined	Marginal Gloss
312 spakly	∴
313 tome	∴
316 lacche	take
328 lodely	∴
328 lures	∴
330 bourne	fountain, water
331 slent	
337 menske alder	
338 rowme	∴
339 heere	praise
344 rottok	∴
347 lethe	∴
350 mellyd	mixed
352 beryd	rang

Glossary

The glossary includes every word and all forms of the words in the edited text. Words occurring frequently are generally marked by + after the third citation. A * against a line-number indicates an emendation. Variation between ȝ and *gh*, þ and *th*, *i* and *y* is not noted. In the alphabetical arrangement ȝ follows *g*, *i* as a consonant (= /j/) follows *i* as a vowel, þ is treated as *th* (so between *te* and *ti*), *v* as a consonant follows *v* as a vowel, *y* as a vowel is treated as *i*. Verbs are given in their infinitive form if that is recorded in the text, and then in the order present tense 1st person singular, 2nd, 3rd; present plural, subjunctive; past tense 1st person, 2nd, 3rd; past tense plural; present participle, past participle.

Abbreviations are: *adj.* adjective, *adv.* adverb, *comp.* comparative, *conj.* conjunction, *gen.* genitive, *imp.* imperative, *impers.* impersonal, *interj.* interjection, *n.* noun, *num.* numeral, *pa.* past tense, *pl.* plural, *pr.* present tense, *prep.* preposition, *pron.* pronoun, *pr. p.* present participle, *pp.* past participle, *sg.* singular, *subj.* subjunctive, *superl.* superlative, *v.* infinitive verb.

Abbreviations used in etymologies are: prec. preceding entry, AN Anglo-Norman, Lat Latin, OE Old English, OF Old French, ON Old Norse. OE etymons are cited in their West Saxon form unless a closer Anglian form is attested. An AN form is given where it is a closer etymon than the OF equivalent. ON etymons are generally given in their Old Icelandic form; for detailed information consult *Gersum*. A * against an etymology indicates an unrecorded form.

a *indef. art.* a 3, 27, 38 +; an 108, 127, 211 [OE *ān*]
abatyd *pp.* demolished 37 [OF *abatre*]
abbay *n.* abbey 108 [AN *abbai*]
aboute *adv.* around, about 48, 56, 110, *prep.* about, concerning 56, 110 [OE *onbūtan*]
abyme *n.* abyss 334 [OF *abi(s)me*]
acounte *n.* reckoning 209 [OF *acounte*]
adoun *adv.* down 322 [OE *of dūne*]

after *adv.* afterwards 112, 116, in the name of 195; *prep.* for, in order to get 126, 304, 307 +, after 141; ~ þat after 207 [OE *æfter*]
afterwarde *adv.* afterwards 127 [OE *æfterwearde*]
age *n.* age 150 [OF *age*]
aghe *n.* dread, awe 234 [ON *agi*]
aghte *num.* eight 210* [OE *eahta*]
aghtene *num.* eighteen 208 [OE *eahtatēne*]
aghtes *pa. 2 sg.* owned, possessed 224; **aghte** *3 sg.* 27* [OE *āgan*]
ay *adv.* always 278, 287, 301 [ON *ei*]
ay-lastande *adj.* everlasting 347 [prec. + OE *læstan*]
al *conj.* although 226 [OE *eall*]
al *adv.* entirely 75, 78, 122 +, **alle** 300 [as prec.]
alder *n.* ancestor 295 [OE *ealdor*]
alder-grattyst *superl. adj.* greatest of all 5; **alder-grattest** 337 [OE *ealra* + *grēat* + *-est*]
al(le) *n.* everyone 54, 310; *adj.* all 10, 23, 63 + [OE *eall*]
allas *adv.* alas 288 [OF *allas*]
alowes *pr. 3 sg.* gives credit for 267 [AN *alower*]
als *see* **as**
also *adv.* also 327, 339 [OE *ealswā*]
altogeder *adv.* entirely 228 [OE *eall* + *tōgædre*]
amounte *v.* reach, be sufficient 284 [OF *amounter*]
and *conj.* and 3, 9, 13 + [OE *and*]
any *adj.* any 85, 206, 284 [OE *ǣnig*]
anoye *n.* suffering 210 [OF *anoye*]
ansuare *n.* answer 127 [OE *andswaru*]
ansuare *imp.* answer 184 [OE *andswarian*]
appull *n.* apple 295 [OE *æppel*]
araide *pp.* dressed 77, **arayed** 271 [AN *arayer*]
are *adv.* before 36 [ON *ár*, OE *ǣr*]
arne, art *see* **be**
art *n.* province 33 [Irish *aird*]
as *adv.* as 91, 139 as if 88, 92, **als** 89, 242; **as ... as** 88, 92, 316 + [OE *al-swā*]
as *conj.* as, just as 4, 36, 183 +, while 43, 45, as if 64, 88, since 135, 182 [as prec.]
aske *pr. pl. subj.* ask 171; **askyd** *pa. 3 sg.* asked 96 [OE *āscian*]
aspied *pa. pl.* saw 65 [OF *espier*]
assent *n.* agreement 66 [OF *assent*]
at *prep.* at 1, 34, 257, 332, among 170 [OE *æt*]
atyrid *pp.* dressed 130 [OF *atirer*]
autere *n.* altar 137 [OF *auter*]
auay *v.* inform 174 [OF *aveier*]
auisyd *pa. pl.* scrutinised 53 [OF *aviser*]
awen *adj.* own 235 [OE *āgen*]

baythes *pr. 3 sg.* questions 257 [ON *beiða*]
bale *n.* sorrow 257, 340 [OE *balu*]
balefully *adv.* sorrowfully 311 [OE *balufull* + *-līce*]
bapteme *n.* baptism 330 [OF *bapteme*]
barones *n. pl.* lords 142 [OF *baron*]
bashis *pr. 3 sg.* disconcerts, puzzles 261 [OF *baissier*]
be *v.* be 94, 97, 180 +; **art** *pr. 2 sg.* 185, 188; **is** *3 sg.* is 25, 146, 147 +; **are** *pl.* 164, 283, 298, 302, **arne** 304; **be** *imp.* 181; *1 sg. subj.* 122; *3 sg.* 324, 325, 326, 327; **wos** *pa. 1 sg.* was 227; *2 sg.* 288; *3 sg.* 11, 31, 73 +, **was** 3, 6, 12 +; *pl.* were 350, **were** 32, 52, 128 +; *subj. sg.* 64, 72, 158 +; **ben(e)** been *pp.* 7, 26, 98 + [OE *bēon* etc.]
bede *pa. 1 sg.* offered 243; **boden** *pp.* offered, exchanged 214 [OE *bēodan*]
bede *see* **bydde**
bedels *n. pl.* city officials 59, 111 [OF *bedel*]
before *prep.* in front of 143, ~ *þat* before 209 [OE *beforan*]
begynnes *pr. 3 sg.* begins 131 [OE *beginnan*]
behalue *n.* behalf 181 [OE *be* + *half*]
belles *n. pl.* bells 352 [OE *belle*]
beme *n.* tree, i.e. the cross 182 [OE *bēam*]
benche *n.* bench, judge's seat 250 [OE *benc*]
bende *pp.* stretched 182 [OE *bendan*]
bere *pa. 3 sg.* bore 326, ~ *doun* lowered 311 [OE *beran*]
beryd *pa. pl.* rang out 352 [? OE *gebǣran*]
besiet *pa. pl.* busied 56 [OE *bysigian*]
besyde *prep.* beside 142 [OE *be sīdan*]
bete *pa. pl.* drove, chased 9; **beten** *pp.* in ~ *doun* knocked down 37 [OE *bēatan*]
better *adv. comp.* more suitably 18; **best** *superl.* best 272 [OE *betera, betst*]
by *prep.* by 71, 90, 121 +, with 66, throughout 31, in term of 157; *adv.* aside 72 [OE *bī*]
bydde *pr. 1 sg.* order 181; **biddes** *3 sg.* 221; **bede** *pa. pl.* 67 [OE *biddan*]
bigripid *pa. 3 sg.* enclosed, encircled 80 [OE *begrīpan*]
byhoues *pr. 3 sg.* must 168 [OE *behōfian*]
biknowe *imp.* make known, reveal 220 [OE *becnāwan*]
bileue *n.* belief 173, 299 [OE *be-* + *gelēafa*]
byschop *n.* bishop 3, 33, 105 +; **bisshop** 193, 221, 257 + [OE *bisceop*]
biseche *v.* beg 120 [OE *besēcan*]
byside *adv.* aside 67 [OE *be sīdan*]
bitan *pp.* assigned to 28 [OE *be-* + ON *taka*]
bytyme *adv.* promptly 112 [OE *bī* + *tīma*]
bitter *adj.* bitter, furious 214* [OE *bitter*]
bitwene *adv.* in between 196; *prep.* between 214 [OE *betwēonum*]
blakke *adj.* black 343 [OE *blæc*]

blee *n.* colour 87, 343 [OE *blēo*]
blynne *v.* stop 111 [OE *blinnan*]
blisful(l) *adj.* glorious 76, 326 [from OE *bliss*]
blysnande *pr. p.* shining 87 [cf. OE *blysian*]
blis(se) *n.* bliss, joy 340, i.e. heaven 345 [OE *bliss*]
blissid *pp.* blest 326, **blessid** 340; *as adj.* blessed, holy 3 [OE *blētsian*]
blo *adj.* dark 290 [ON *blár*]
blode *n.* blood 182, 290 [OE *blōd*]
blonke *n.* horse 112 [OE *blanca*]
bode *n.* bidding, command 181, **boode** 193 [OE *bod*]
boden *see* **bede**
bodeword *n.* message, news 105 [OE *bod* + *word*]
body *n.* body 76, 94, 106 + [OE *bodig*]
bogh *v.* be obedient 194; **boghit** *pa. pl.* went 59 [OE *būgan*]
boghtes *pa. 2 sg.* redeemed 289 [OE *bycgan*]
boke *n.* book 103* [OE *bōc*]
bolde *adj.* great 106, brave 213 [OE *bald*]
bone *n.¹* request 194 [ON *bón*]
bone *n.²* slayer 243 [OE *bana*]
bone *adj.* obedient 181 [ON *búinn*]
bones *n. pl.* bones 346 [OE *bān*]
bonkes *n. pl.* shores 32 [ON *bakki*, from **banke*]
boode *see* **bode**
bordure *n.* border of shield 51; **bordures** *pl.* ornamental borders of dress 82 [OF *bordure*]
bot *adv.* merely, just 32, *not* ~ only 194, 208; *conj.* but 52, 54, 73 +, (after neg.) anything other than 97, unless 99, 158 146 [OE *būte*]
bote *n.* remedy 170, 327 [OE *bōt*]
bothe *adj.* both 194 [ON *báðir*]
bothum *n.* bottom 76 [OE *botm*]
bounty *n.* in *to* ~ as an honour 248 [OF *bounté*]
bourne *n.* river, stream 330 [OE *burna*]
brayed *pa. 3 sg.* stirred 190 [OE *bregdan*]
brawnche *n.* part, share 276 [OF *braunche*]
breuyt *pp.* spoken 103 [OE *gebrēfan*]
bry3t *adj.* bright 51, 87, 330, fair 190 [OE *beorht*]
bryng *v.* in ~ *hom in wordes* make words of them, interpret them 56; **bro3t** *pa. pl.* drove 9; **broght** *pp.* brought 105, 340 [OE *bringan*]
brode *adj.* broad 55 [OE *brāde*]
brothire *n.* brother 213 [OE *brōþor*]
buggid *pp.* built 37, 207 [ON *byggva*]
burde *pa. impers.* in *hom* ~ it was necessary for them to, they ought to 260 [OE *gebyrian*]

burgeys *n. pl.* citizens 59 [OF *burgeis*]
burgh *n.* town 3, 207, 352, *in* ~ among people 103 [OE *burg*]
buriet *pa. pl.* buried 248, **buried** *pp.* 94, 106 [OE *byrgan*]
burynes *n.* burial place, tomb 142, 190 [OE *byrignes*]
buskyd *pa. 3 sg.* hurried 112 [ON *búask*]
busmare *n.* vilification, abuse 214 [OE *bīsmer*]

ca3t *see* **kaghten**
cayser *n.* emperor 199 [Lat *Caesar*, OE *cāsere*]
callid *pa. 3 sg.* called 16 [ON *kalla*]
camelyn *n.* camel hair, fine material 82 [AN *camelin*]
careles *adj.* generous 172 [OE *carlēas*]
carpe *v.* speak 317 [ON *karpa*]
cast *v.* cast, throw 317; **kest** *pp.* placed 83 [ON *kasta*]
cause *n.* reason 220; **causes** *pl.* legal actions 202 [OF *cause*]
cenacle *n.* chamber, room 336 [OF *cēnacle*]
cessyd *pa. 3 sg.* ceased 341; *pp.* ended 136 [OF *cesser*]
chargit *pa. 3 sg.* placed under care 18 [OF *charger*]
chaungit *pa. 3 sg.* changed 18 [OF *changer*]
chere *n.* face 342 [OF *chere*]
cheuely *adv.* at once 18 [OF *chef* + OE *līce*]
childes *n. gen.* child's 318 [OE *cild*]
cité *n.* city 201 [OF *cité*]
cladden *pa. pl.* clothed 249 [OE *clæþan*]
clansyd *pa. 3 sg.* cleansed 16 [OE *clǣnsian*]
clene *adj.* elegant 82, unspoilt 259 [OE *clǣne*]
clerke *n.* cleric 55 [late OE *clerc* from OF]
cloyster *n.* enclosed area 140 [OF *cloistre*]
clos *n.* cathedral precinct 55 [OF *clos*]
cloth(e) *n.* cloth 82, clothing 148, 263, 266; **clothes** *pl.* garments 259 [OE *clāþ*]
cloutes *n. pl.* rags 259 [OE *clūt*]
clustrede *pp. adj.* bunched 140* [from OE *clyster*]
coyfe *n.* coif, lawyer's cap 83 [OF *coife*]
colde *adv.* sadly 305 [OE *calde*]
colour(e) *n.* colour 148, 263 [OF *colour*]
comaundit *pa. 3 sg.* commanded 115 [OF *comaunder*]
come *v.* in ~ *to* manage 74; *pa. 3 sg.* came 113, 142; **commen** *pa. pl.* came 63 [OE *cuman*]
comforth(e) *n.* comfort, support 168, 172 [OF *confort*]
committid *pp.* commissioned 201 [AN *committer*, Lat *committere*]
communnates *n. pl.* communities 14 [OF *comunité*]
con *pr. pl.* can 156; **couthe** *pa. 3 sg.* could 100, 101, did 249 [OE *cunnan*]
confirmyng *n.* corroboration of 124 [OF *confirmer*]

confourmyd *pa. 3 sg.* conformed to, agreed with 242 [OF *conformer*]
consciens *n.* conscience 237 [OF *conscience*]
conuertyd *pa. 3 sg.* converted 14 [OF *convertir*]
corce *see* cors
corners *n. pl.* corners 71 [AN *corner*]
coron *see* croun
coronyd *pa. pl.* crowned 254 [OF *coroner*]
corrupt *adj.* decomposed 346 [OF *corrupt*, Lat *corruptus*]
cors *n.* corpse 110, 317, **corce** 177 [OF *cors*]
councele *imp.* conceal 184 [OF *conceler*]
counsell *n.* wisdom, understanding 167, 266, advice 172 [OF *counseil*]
courte *n.* lawcourt 249 [OF *court*]
couthe *see* con
couthely *adv.* evidently 98 [OE *cūplīce*]
couert *pa. 3 sg.* covered 346 [OF *covrir*]
couetise *n.* avarice 237 [OF *coveitise*]
crafte *n.* skill, power 167, (created) material 346 [OE *cræft*]
crafty *adj.* skilful, learned 44 [OE *cræftig*]
crakit *pa. 3 sg.* resounded 110 [OE *cracian*]
creatore *n.* creator 168 [AN *creator*]
creatures *gen. pl.* creatures', i.e. humans' 167 [AN *creatur*]
cry *n.* outcry 110 [OF *cri*]
Cristen *adj.* Christian 124, 209 [OE *cristen*, from Lat]
Cristendome *n.* Christianity 2, **Cristendame** 14 [OE *cristendōm*]
cronicle *n.* historical account 156; **cronecles** *pl.* 44 [AN *cronicle*]
crosse *n.* cross 2 [ON *kross*]
croun *n.* crown 222, **coron** 83; **crownes** *pl.* clerical tonsures 55 [OF *coro(u)ne*]
crowes *n. pl.* crowbars 71 [OE *crāwe*]
cumely *adj.* attractive 82* [OE *cȳmelic*]
cure *n.* remedy 168 [OF *cure*]
curtest *adj. superl.* most gracious 249 [OF *curteis* + -*est*]

day *n.* day 236; **dayes** *pl.* 155, **dawes** 7 [OE *dæg*]
day-belle *n.* morning bell 117 [OE *dæg* + *belle*]
dalfe *pa. pl.* dug 45; **doluen** *pp.* buried 99 [OE *delfan*]
dampnyd *pp.* condemned 302 [OF *dampner*]
date *n.* period of time 205 [OF *date*]
daungerde *pa. 3 sg.* implicated 320 [OF *dangerer*]
dawes *pr. 3 sg.* dawns 306; **dawid** *pa. 3 sg.* grew light 127 [OE *dagian*]
dawes *see* day
debonerté *n.* graciousness, goodness 123 [OF *deboneretē*]
declynet *pa. 3 sg.* turned aside, deviated 237 [OF *decliner*]
dede *n.*1 dead person, corpse 116 [OE *dēad*]

dede *n.*2 business, job 169 [OE *dǣd*]
dede *adj.* dead 225, 309, 320 [OE *dēad*]
dedifie *v.* dedicate, consecrate 6; **dedifiet** *pa. 3 sg.* 23 [OF *dediier* and *edifiier*]
defaute *n.* damage, injury 148 [OF *defaute*]
deghed *pa. 1 sg.* died 246 [ON *deyja*]
dene *n.* dean 144 [OF *deien*]
denyed *pa. 3 sg.* dinned, resounded 246 [OE *dynian*]
depe *adj.* deep 302 [OE *dēop*]
depe *adv.* deeply 45, 99 [OE *dēope*]
deputate *n.* deputy 227 [Lat *deputatus*]
dere, deere *adj.* precious, beloved, honoured 23, 123, 144 +, welcome 193; **derrest** *superl.* most beloved 29 [OE *dēore*]
derfe *adj.* great 99 [ON *djarfr*]
derke *adj.* dark 117, 294, 306 [OE *deorc*]
deth(e) *n.* death 294, 306 [OE *dēaþ*]
deuel(l) *n.* devil 15, 27 [OE *dēofol*]
deuyne *pr. pl. subj.* speculate 169 [OF *deviner*]
deuyse *v.* explain 225; **deuysit** *pa. 3 sg.* described 144, 309 [OF *deviser*]
deuoydes *pr. 3 sg.* removes, gets rid of 348; **deuoydit** *pa. 3 sg.* departed, went away 116 [OF *devoidier*]
dyght, dy3t *pa. 3 sg.* made over, assigned 23, 294; *pl.* worked 45 [OE *dihtan*]
digne *pr. 3 sg. subj.* grant 123 [OF *deinier*]
dymly *adv.* miserably 306* [OE *dimlīc*]
ditte *pa. 3 sg.* shut 116 [OE *dyttan*]
dyuerse *adj.* different 60 [OF *divers*]
do *pr. pl. subj.* let us do 169 [OE *dōn*]
dole *n.* part 6 [OE *dāl*]
doluen *see* **dalfe**
dome *n.* judgement 236 [OE *dōm*]
domesmon *n.* judge 227 [from prec.]
doun *adv.* down 6, 311, 320 [OE *of dūne*]
drawen *pp.* pulled 6 [OE *dragan*]
drede *n.* fear 233 [from OE *drǣdan*]
dreme *n.* sound 191 [OE *drēam*]
drery *adj.* mournful 191 [OE *drēorig*]
dresse *v.* prepare, deliver 236 [OF *drecier*]
dryghtyn *n.* god 29 [OE *dryhten*]
dryues *pr. 3 sg.* in ~ owte sends out, utters 191 [OE *drīfan*]
droppyd *pa. 2 sg.* dropped 320 [OE *dropian*]
duke *n.* leader 227 [OF *duc*]
dul *n.* sorrow 246 [OF *dul*]
dulfully *adv.* miserably 302, 309 [from prec.]
durre *n.* door 116 [OE *duru*]

dwellid *pa. pl.* lived 10 [OE *dwellan*]
dwynande *pr. p.* languishing, pining 294 [OE *dwīnan*]

efte *adv.* again 37 [OE *eft*]
eggite *pp. adj.* sharp-edged 40* [from OE *ecg*]
eghen *n. pl.* eyes 311, 321, 330, *for myn* ~ on my life 194 [OE *ēage*]
egh-lyddes *n. pl.* eyelids 178 [OE *ēage* + *hlid*]
elles *adv.* otherwise, something else 121 [OE *elles*]
enbawmyd *pp.* embalmed 261, 265 [OF *embaumer*]
enbelicit *pp.* embellished 51 [OF *embellir*]
ende *n.* end 136 [OE *ende*]
enioynyd *pp.* appointed 216 [OF *enjoindre*]
enprise *n.* achievement 253 [OF *enprise*]
entouchid *pp.* poisoned 297 [OF *entochier*]
er(e) *adv.* previously 19, 24, before 118, 308 [OE *ǣr*]
eres *n. pl.* ears 90 [OE *ēare*]
erth(e) *n.* earth 45, the Earth 196, 198, *on* ~ worldly 237, anywhere 250 [OE *eorþe*]
ete *pa. 3 sg.* ate 295 [OE *etan*]
euel *adv.* hardly 276 [OE *yfel*]
euer *adv.* ever 103, 198, 255, always 230, 256, 288, *for* ~ for all time 154, 296, 338 [OE *ǣfre*]
euermore *adv.* ever since 26, all the time 110 [OE *ǣfre mā*]
exilid *pp.* exiled 303 [AN *exiler*]

face *n.* face 89, 323 [OF *face*]
fader *n.* father 244, 294; *gen.* 243, 318 [OE *fæder*]
faylid *pa. 3 sg.* was lacking in 287, vanished 342 [OF *faillir*]
fayne *adj.* ready, eager 176 [OE *fægen*]
faith(e) *n.* Christian faith 13, 124, 173, pagan faith 204, 242, *gode* ~ trustworthiness 230, honesty 252 [OF *feid*]
faitheful *adj.* faithful 299 [from prec.]
faitheles *adj.* without faith 287 [from OF *feid*]
fals *adj.* false, corrupt 231, 244 [OE *fals*, from Lat *falsus*]
fastynge *n.* confirming 173 [from OE *fæstan*]
fauour *n.* favour, partiality 244 [OF *favour*]
fell *pa. impers.* it befell 244; **felle** *pa. 3 sg.* fell 323 [OE *feallan*]
felonse *adj.* treacherous 231 [OF *felons*]
ferforthe *adv.* far 242 [OE *feorr* + *forþ*]
ferly *n.* wonder, marvel 145 [from ON *ferligr*]
ferly *adv.* wonderfully 46 [ON *ferliga*]
feste *n.* feast 303* [OF *feste*]
fife *adj.* five 208 [OE *fīf*]

Glossary 119

fynde *v.* find 156; **founden** *pa. pl.* found 43, 46 [OE *findan*]
fyndynge *n.* discovery 145 [from prec.]
fyne *adj.* genuine 173; **fynest** *superl.* most excellent 252 [OF *fin*]
fynger *n.* finger 145, 165 [OE *finger*]
fyrre *adv. comp.* further 169, 293 [OE *firra*]
fyrst *adj.* first 331; *adv.* firstly 197 [OE *fyrest*]
fyrst(e) *n.* in *on* ~ first of all 42, 207, at once 144* [as prec.]
flesh *n.* flesh, skin 89 [OE *flǣsc*]
flore *n.* flat surface 46 [OE *flōr*]
folke *n.* people 231 [OE *folc*]
folowid *pa. pl.* followed 351 [OE *folgian*]
folwe *pr. 1 sg.* baptise 318 [OE *fulwian*]
fonte *n.* font 299 [OE *font*, from Lat]
for *prep.* because of, on account of 215, 237, 246 +, for the sake of 132, 233, 234, as 222, 249, 250 +, ~ *to* to 40, 41, in order to 236 [OE *for*]
for *conj.* for, because 7, 29, 45 + [as prec.]
forgo *v.* avoid 275 [OE *forgān*]
forthe *adv.* forth 351 [OE *forþ*]
forþi *adv.* therefore 279 [OE *forþī*]
forwrast *pp.* seized, overcome 220 [OE *for-* + *wrǣstan*]
fote *n.* footings 42 [OE *fōt*]
founden *see* **fynde**
fourme *n.* in *in* ~ *of* in accordance with 230 [OF *fourme*]
fourmyt *pp.* constructed 46 [OF *fourmer*]
fourty *adj.* forty 230 [OE *fēowertig*]
fre *adj.* noble, gracious 318 [OE *frēo*]
freke *n.* man 287, 323 [OE *freca*]
frende *n.* friend 176 [OE *frēond*]
freshe *adj.* fresh, undecayed 89 [OF *fresche*]
fro *prep.* from 12, 107, 116 + [ON *frá*]
frowarde *adj.* recalcitrant, unruly 231 [ON *frá* + OE *-weard*]
fulfille *v.* fulfil 176 [OE *fullfyllan*]
ful(l) *adv.* very 1, 53, 55 + [OE *full*]
fulloght *n.* baptism 299 [OE *fullwiht*]
fulsen *pr. 3 sg. subj.* help 124 [OE *filst* + *-en*]
fundement *n.* foundations 42 [OF *fondement*]
furrit *pp.* trimmed with fur 81, **furrid** provided with a fur-trimmed garment 252 [OF *furrer*]

gay *adj.* bright 75, handsome 134 [OF *gai*]
gargeles *n. pl.* gargoyles, decorative carvings 48 [OF *gargouille*]
garnysht *pp.* decorated 48 [OF *garnir, garniss-*]
gate *n.* path 241 [ON *gata*]

gedrid *pp.* gathered 134 [OE *gadrian*]
gentile *adj.* pagan 216*, 229* [Lat *gentīlis*]
gete *pa. 3 sg.* got, i.e. persuaded 241 [ON *geta*]
gyfe *v.* give 276; **gefe** *pa. 3 sg.* 282 [OE *gifan*, ON *gefa*]
gynful *adj.* dishonest, deceitful 238 [from OF *engin*]
gynge *n.* company 137 [ON *gengi*]
glent *v.* swerve, deviate 241 [? cf. ON *glettr*]
glisnande *pr. p.* glowing 78 [OE *glisnian*]
glode *n.* space? 75 [uncertain]
glotte *n.* filth, corruption 297 [OF *glette*]
glow *pr. pl. subj.* cry out 171 [OE *gleowian*]
god(de) *n.* God 171, 282, 325 +; *gen.* **goddes** 316 [OE *god*]
gode *n.* good 230 [OE *gōd*]
golde *n.* gold 80, 248, gold paint 75, gold thread 78; *adj.* golden 51 [OE *gold*]
goste *n.* spirit 192, Holy ~ Holy Spirit 127, 319, ~*-lyfe* spirit-life [OE *gāst*]
gouernour *n.* governor 251 [OF *governeor*]
gowne *n.* gown 78 [OF *goune*]
grace *n.* grace 120, 126, 171 + [OF *grace*]
gracious *adj.* gracious 319 [OF *gracious*]
gray *adj.* shining grey 48 [OE *grǣg*]
graythist *adj. superl.* most powerful 251 [ON *greiðr*]
graue *n.* grave 153 [OE *græf*]
graunte *n.* in ~ *hade* received a favour 126 [OF *grant*]
grete *n.* earth 41 [OE *grēot*]
grete *adj.* great 134, 141, 282 + [OE *grēat*]
grette *pa. 3 sg.* wept 126 [OE *grētan*]
gronyng *n.* groan 282 [from OE *grānian*]
grounde *n.* solid ground 41 [OE *grund*]
grubber *n.* digger 41 [cf. OE **grybban*]
grue *n.* bit 319 [OF *gru*]
gurden *pa. pl.* girded, equipped with a belt 251 [OE *gyrdan*]
gurdill *n.* belt 80 [OE *gyrdel*]

ȝea *adv.* yes 273 [OE *gǣ*]
ȝe(e) *pron.* you 170, 175, 297 +; **ȝow** *acc.* 174; **ȝour** *gen.* your 173, 176, 209 [OE *gē* etc.]
ȝemyd *pa. 1 sg.* governed 202 [OE *gēman*]
ȝepely *adv.* skilfully 88 [OE *gēap + līce*]
ȝeres *n. pl.* years 11, **ȝere** (after numeral) 208, 210 [OE *gēar*]
ȝet *adv.* still 44, 257, even so 148, even 199, *and* ~ plus 210 [OE *gēt*]
ȝisturday *n.* yesterday 88 [OE *gestrandæg*]
ȝode *pa. 3 sg.* went, walked 198 [OE *ēode*]
ȝorde *n.* precinct, churchyard 88 [OE *geard*]

Glossary 121

ȝoskyd *pa. 3 sg.* sobbed 312 [OE *geocsian*]
ȝour, ȝow *see* ȝe(e)

had(e) *see* haue
halde *v.* hold, support 42, 166, **holde** preside over 249; **haldes** *pr. 2 sg.* 223 [OE *haldan*]
halowes *n. pl.* saints 23 [OE *hālga*]
han *see* haue
harde *adj.* hard 40, 288 [OE *heard*]
harmes *n. pl.* injuries 232 [OE *hearm*]
hathel *n.* person 198 [cf. OE *hæleþ*]
hatte *pa. 3 sg.* was called 4, 25, 38 [OE *hātan*]
haue *v.* have 260; **has** *pr. 2 sg.* 187, 195; *3 sg.* has 147; *pl.* 148, **haue** 155, 271*, **han** 300; **hades** *pa. 2 sg.* possessed 224, 315; **had(e)** *3 sg.* had 7, 95, 119 +, ~ **hym in** brought in, installed 17; **haden** *pl.* had 8 [OE *habban*]
he *pron.* he 13, 15, 17 +; **him** 142, 204, 258 +, (to) him 121, himself 129; **his** 5, 28, 65 +, **hise** 174* [OE *hē* etc.]
hedde *n.* head 281 [OE *hēafod*]
heere *v.* praise 339; **herid** *pp.* 325 [OE *herian*]
hegh *adj.* high 325, 339, ~ **masse** 129, noble 137, true 241; **heghest** *superl.* supreme 253; *adv.* high 223 [OE *hēh*]
heire *n.* heir, inheritor 211 [OF *eir*]
heldes *pr. pl.* bow 196; **heldyt** *pa. 3 sg.* passed 137 [OE *heldan*]
helle *n.* hell 196; **helle-hole** pit of hell 291, 307 [OE *helle*]
hemmyd *pp.* bordered 78 [from OE *hemm* n.]
hende *adj.* worthy 58, 325 [OE *gehende*]
hent *pa. 1 sg.* received 232; **hentes** *2 sg.* seized 291 [OE *hentan*]
herden *pa. pl.* heard 310 [OE *hēran*]
here *adv.* here 13, 146, 157 + [OE *hēr*]
herghdes *pa. 2 sg.* harrowed 291 [OE *hergian*]
herid *see* heere
herken *v.* hear 134, ~ **after** look out for 307 [OE *hercnian*]
herte *n.* heart, conscience 242*, 257* [OE *heorte*]
hethen *adj.* heathen, pagan 7 [OE *hǣþen*]
heuen *n.* heaven 166, 196 [OE *heofon*]
hewe *v.* cut 40; **hewen** *pp.* carved 47 [OE *hēawan*]
hewes *n. pl.* hues 87 [OE *hēow*]
hyder *adv.* to this place 8 [OE *hider*]
highid *pa. pl.* hurried 58 [OE *hīgian*]
him, his *see* he
hit *pron.* it 7, 26, 31 +, (with pl. v. **arne**) they are 304; *gen.* its 309 [OE *hit*]
ho *pron.* she 274, 279, 308, 326; **hyr** her 308, 337, 338, to her 280 [OE *hēo, hire*]
holde *see* halde

holy *adj.* holy 4, 319 [OE *hālig*]
hom *pron.* them 16, 23, 53 +, themselves 56; **hor** their 17, 18, 61 + (*and see* þai) [OE *heom, heora*]
home *n.* home 107 [OE *hām*]
honde *n.* hand 84, 223, **hondes** *pl.* 90, 166 [OE *hond*]
honde-quile *n.* short time, instant 64 [OE *hondhwīl*]
honesté *n.* honesty 253 [OF *honesté*]
hongyt *pp.* hanged 244 [ON *hengja*, OE *hōn*]
honour *n.* in *for þe* ~ in honour of 253 [OF *honour*]
hope *pr. 1 sg.* believe 4 [OE *hopian*]
hor *see* **hom**
houre *n.* hour 326; **houres** *pl.* devotions at canonical hours 119 [OF *ure*]
how *adv.* how 95, 147, 187 + [OE *hū*]
hummyd *pa. 3 sg.* murmured 281 [echoic]
hundrid, hundred *n.* hundred 58, 208 [OE *hundred*]
hungride *pa. pl.* hungered 304 [OE *hyngran*]
hungrie *adj.* hungry 307 [OE *hungrig*]
hurlyd *pa. 3 sg.* threw 17 [uncertain]

I *pron.* I 122, 201, 285 +; **me** 124, 195, 241 +, to me 193; **my** 123, 184, 205 +; **myn** 194, 235, 253; **myselfe** I myself 197, 300 [OE *ic, mē, mīn*]
ydols *n. pl.* idols 17, 29 [OF *idole*]
if *conj.* if 176, 274, even if 271 [OE *gif*]
ylka *adj.* every 96 [OE *ylc* + *ān*]
ilke *adj.* in *þat / þis* ~ that/this (emphatic) 101, 193 [OE *ilca*]
in *prep.* in 1, 3, 5 +, among 109, 217, into 259, 260 [OE *in*]
inne *prep.* (postpositional) inside 149, in 326*, within 328* [OE *inne*]
into *prep.* into 9, 12, 45 + [OE *in tō*]
inwith *prep.* within 307 [OE *in* + *wið*]
yrne *n.* iron 71 [OE *īren*]
is *see* **be**

iapes *n. pl.* tricks, fraudulent decisions 238 [from OF *japer*]
ioy *n.* joy, glory 180, 188 [OF *joie*]
ioyned *pp.* appointed, assigned 188 [OF *joindre*]
ioly *adj.* lovely, fine 229 [OF *jolif*]
iuge *n.* judge 216 [OF *juge*]
iugement *n.* judgement, decision 238 [OF *jugement*]
iuggit *pp.* decreed 180, **iuggid** condemned 188 [OF *juger*]
iustifiet *pa. 1 sg.* administered justice 229 [OF *justifier*]
iustises *n. pl.* judges 254 [OF *justice*]

kaghten *pa. pl.* caught 71; **caȝt** *pp.* acquired, received 148 [AN *cacher*]
keies *n. pl.* keys 140 [OE *cǣg*]

kene *adj.* prudent, wise 254 [OE *cēne*]
kenely *adv.* (as intensive) very 63 [OE *cēnlīce*]
kenne *v.* make known, explain 124 [OE *cennan*]
kepten *pa. pl.* took charge of 66; kepyd *pp.* kept 266 [OE *cēpan*]
kest *see* cast
kydde *pp.* made known, recorded 44, recognised 222; kidde *adj.* illustrious, renowned 113, 254 [from OE *cȳþan*]
kynde *n.* nature, natural signs 157 [OE *(ge)cynd*]
kyng(e) *n.* king 98, 156, 199 + [OE *cyning*]
kynned *pa. 3 sg.* was born 209 [cf. OE *(ge)cennan*]
kynnes *n. pl.* kinds 63 [OE *cynn*]
kyrke *n.* church 113; kyrkes *pl.* 16 [ON *kirkja*]
kith *n.* country 98 [OE *cȳþ*]
kny3t *n.* knight 199 [OE *cniht*]
knowe *v.* understand 74; *pr. 1 sg.* know 263; knewe *pa. 3 sg.* 285 [OE *cnāwan*]

lacche *v.* fetch 316 [OE *læccan*]
lady *n.* in oure ~ the Virgin Mary 21 [OE *hlǣfdige*]
laddes *n. pl.* boys, servants 61 [uncertain]
laftes *pa. 2 sg.* left 292; laften *pl.* abandoned 61 [OE *lǣfan*]
lagh(e) *n.* doctrine, faith 34, religious system 187, (pagan) faith 203*, law 200, 245, lawe 216; laghes *pl.* behaviours, practices 268, God's laws, doctrines 287 [late OE *lagu*, from ON]
lay *v.* lay, set 67; laide *pa. pl.* set 72, laid, placed 149 [OE *lecgan*]
lay, layn(e) *see* lye
layne *imp.* remain silent 179 [ON *leyna*]
laitid *pp.* searched 155 [ON *leita*]
lake *n.* pit 302 [OE *lac*, Lat *lacus*]
lant *see* lene
large *adj.* large 72 [OF *large*]
lasse *adv.* less 320, more ne ~ in any way, at all 104; *n.* in þe more and the ~ people of all ranks 247 [OE *lǣssa*]
lasshit *pa. 3 sg.* flashed 334 [? imitative]
last(e) *v.* last, endure 264*, 272; lastyd *pa. 3 sg.* 215 [OE *lǣstan*]
later *comp. adj.* in ~ ende latter part 136 [OE *later*]
lathe *v.* invite 308 [OE *laþian*]
lauande *pr. p.* flowing 314 [OE *lafian* and OF *laver*]
lawe(s) *see* lagh(e)
lede *n.* man 146, 150, 200 + [OE *lēod*]
lege men *n. pl.* vassals 224 [OF *lege*]
lely *adv.* faithfully, sincerely 268 [From OF *leel*]
leme *n.* gleam 334 [OE *lēoma*]
lene *pr. 3 sg. subj.* grant 315; lant *pp. adj.* granted 192, 272 [OE *lǣnan*]

lenger *see* **long(e)**
lengyd *pa. 3 sg.* remained 68 [OE *lengan*]
lengthe *n.* extent of time 205 [OE *lengþu*]
lepen *pa. pl.* ran 61 [OE *hlēapan*]
lere *n.* features 95 [ON *hlýr*, OE *hlēor*]
leste *n.* least 162 [OE *lǣst*]
lethe *v.* end 347 [uncertain]
lettes *pr. 3 sg.* hinders 165 [OE *lettan*]
lettres *n. pl.* letters, written characters 51, written orders 111 [OF *lettre*]
leue *n.* permission 316 [OE *lēaf*]
leue *v.* believe 175, 176; **leues** *pr. pl.* 176; **leuen** 183 [OE *gelēfan*]
leuyd *see* **lyuye**
lewid *adj.* unknown (?) 205 [OE *lǣwede*]
librarie *n.* library 155 [OF *librairie*]
lyche *n.* body 146, 314 [OE *līc*]
lidde *n.* lid 67, 72 [OE *hlid*]
lye *v.* lie 264; **ligges** *pr. 2 sg.*186; **lyes** 3 *sg.* 99, 179; **lyggid** *pa. 3 sg.* 76, lay 281, 314; **layn(e)** *pp.* lain, been lying 95, 147, 157 + [OE *licgan*]
lyfe *n.* life 192, 315, 347, **lyue** 236, *opon* ~ alive 150, ~ *ne lym* i.e. body nor soul 224 [OE *līf*]
lyftand *pr. p.* raising 178 [ON *lyfta*]
ligges, lyggid *see* **lye**
lighten *pa. pl.* fall 322 [OE *līhtan*]
liȝtly *adv.* brightly 334 [OE *lēohtlīce*]
lying *n.* lying dead 205 [from OE *licgan*]
lykhame *n.* body 179 [OE *līchama*]
lym *n.* limb 224 [OE *lim*]
limbo *n.* limbo 292 [Lat *in limbo*, from *limbus*]
lippes *n. pl.* lips 91 [OE *lippa*]
lire *n.* flesh 149 [OE *līra*]
listonde *pa. pl.* listened 219 [OE *hlysnan*]
litell *n.* little 160, 190; **litell(e)** *adv.* little 165, 348 [OE *lȳtel*]
lyue *see* **lyfe**
lyuye *v.* live 298; **leuyd** *pp.* 328 [OE *lifian*]
lo *interj.* look 146 [OE *lā*]
lodely *adj.* horrible 328 [OE *lāþlic*]
loffynge *n.* remnant, remainder 292 [from OE *lāf*]
lofte *n.* in *on* ~ above 81 [*see* **olofte**]
logh(e) *adv.* low 334; *as n.* in *on* ~ down below 147 [ON *lágr*]
loke *v.* look 68, observe 157; **lokyd** *pa. 3 sg.* 313 [OE *lōcian*]
loken *pp.* enclosed 147 [OE *lūcan*]
lome *n.* receptacle, i.e. coffin 68, 149 [OE *lōma*]
londe *n.* country 200, land 224; **londes** *pl.* lands 30 [OE *land*]

long *n.* in *vpon* ~ at length, finally 175 [OE *long* adj.]
long *adj.* long 155, ~ *age* great age 150 [as prec.]
long(e) *adv.* long 1, 95, 260 +, for a long time 97*, 126, 147 +; **lenger** *comp.* longer 179, 319 [OE *longe*]
longen *pr. pl.* belong, are affiliated to 268 [cf. OE *gelang*]
lord(e) *n.* lord 134, i.e. God 123, 175, 280 +; **lordes** *pl.* 138, 146 [OE *hlāford*]
lore *n.* learning, skill 264 [OE *lār*]
louse *v.* release, set free 165; **loused** *pa. 3 sg.* uttered (words) 178 [from ON *lauss*]
loue *adj.* beloved 34 [OE *lēof*]
loves *n. pl.* hands 349 [ON *lófi*]
loues *pr. 3 sg.* loves 268, 272 [OE *lufian*]
louyd *pp.* worshipped, glorified 288, 324 [OE *lofian*]
louyng *adj.* praising 349 [from prec.]
lures *n. pl.* losses, deprivations 328 [OE *lyre*]
luste *v. impers.* it pleases 162 [OE *lystan*]

macers *n. pl.* mace bearers 143 [OF *maissier*]
made *see* **make**
maghty *adj.* mighty, powerful 27, 143, 283, **my3ty** almighty 175 [OE *mæhtig, mihtig*]
may *pr. 1 sg.* may; *3 sg.* is able to 151, 293; *pl.* 175; **my3t** *pa. 3 sg.* might, could 94, 97, 258 +; *pl.* were able 74, 166 [OE *mæg*]
maire *n.* mayor 65, 143 [OF *maire*]
mayster-mon *n.* chief official 201 [OF *maistre*, OE *mægester* + OE *man*]
mayster-toun *n.* chief town 26 [prec. + OE *tun*]
maystrie *n.* power, force 234 [OF *maistrie*]
make *v.* make, arrive at 238, ~ *of* calculate, reckon up 206; **makkyd** *pa. pl.* built 43; **makyd** *pp.* in ~ *opon* opened 128, **made** made, set 39, constructed 50, appointed 201, ~ *for to lyuye* restored to life 298 [OE *macian*]
maker *n.* creator 283 [from prec.]
malte *v.* melt away, vanish 158 [OE *gemæltan*]
manas *n.* threat 240 [OF *manase*]
manerly *adv.* in accordance with ritual, ceremoniously 131 [from next]
maners *n. pl.* kinds 60 [AN *manere*]
mantel *n.* robe 81, 250 [OF *mantel*]
marbre *n.* marble 48, 50 [OF *marbre*]
marciall *n.* steward 337 [AN *mareschal*]
martilage *n.* burial register 154 [Lat *martilogium*]
mason *n.* stone-worker 39 [OF *mason*]
masse *n.* mass 129, 131 [OE *mæsse*]
matens *n. pl.* matins 128 [OF *matines*]

matyd *pp.* overcome 163 [OF *mater*]
me *see* **I**
meche *adj.* great 81, much, 206, 220, 350, **mecul** great 27, 286 [OE *mycel*, ON *mykill*]
mede *n.* reward 234; **medes** *pl.* merits, virtues 270 [OE *mēd*]
medecyn *n.* medicine 298 [OF *medecine*]
meeles *n. pl.* meals 307 [OE *mēl*]
meere *n.* place 114 [OE *gemǣre*]
meynye *n.* retinue 65 [OF *menie*]
mekest *adj. superl.* most merciful 250 [ON *mjúkr*]
mellyd *pp.* mingled 350 [OF *meller*]
memorie *n.* historical record 44, memory 158 [OF *memorie*]
men *see* **mon**
mendyd *pp.* cured, healed 298 [AN *mender*]
mene *v.* mean, signify 54, recall 151 [OE *mǣnan*]
menyd *pa. pl.* lamented 247 [OE *mǣnan*]
menyuer *n.* miniver, squirrel fur [AN *menever*, from OF *menu vair*]
menske *n.* honour 337 [ON *mennska*]
menskefully *adv.* beautifully 50 [from prec.]
menskes *pr. 3 sg.* honours 269; **menskid** *pa. pl.* honoured 258 [as prec.]
mercy *n.* mercy 284, 286 [OF *merci*]
merciles *adj.* unforgiven 300 [from prec.]
mery *adj.* lively 39 [OE *myrige*]
meritorie *adj.* meritorious, praiseworthy 270 [OF *meritoire*]
merkid *pp.* recorded 154 [ON *merkja*]
meruayle *n.* marvellous thing 43, 65, 114 + [OF *merveil*]
meschefe *n.* trouble 240 [OF *meschief*]
mesters-mon *n.* craftsman 60 [OF *mester* + OE *man*]
mesure *n.* extent 286 [OF *mesure*]
metely *adv.* fittingly, attractively 50 [from OE *gemǣte*]
metropol *n.* metropolis 26 [OF *metropole*]
mette *pa. 3 sg.* met 337; **metten** *pl.* 114 [OE *mētan*]
my *see* **I**
mydell *n.* waist 80 [OE *middel*]
my3t *n.* power 163; **my3tes** *pl.* 162, 283 [OE *miht*]
my3t *see* **may**
my3ty *see* **maghty**
myn *see* **I**
mynde *n.* memory 97*, 151, 154, mental powers 163 [OE *gemynd*]
mynyd *pa. pl.* excavated 43 [OF *miner*]
ministres *n. pl.* priests 131 [OF *ministre*]
mynnyd *pp.* recalled, mentioned 104 [ON *minna*]
mynnyng *n.* keeping in mind 269 [from prec.]

mynster *n.* minster 27 [OE *mynster*]
mynster-dores *n. pl.* doors to the minster 128 [as prec. + OE *duru*]
mynte *pa. 3 sg.* pointed to 145 [OE *myntan*]
myrthe *see* **murthe**
myselfe *see* **I**
myste *v.* missed, gone without 300 [OE *missan*]
mysterie *n.* mystery 125 [Lat *mysterium*]
mo *adj.* more 210 [OE *mā*]
moder *n.* mother, i.e. Mary 325 [OE *mōdor*]
moght-freten *pp.* moth-eaten 86 [OE *moþþe* + *fretan*]
molde *n.* in *on* ~ in the world 270; **moldes** *pl.* lumps of earth 343 [OE *molde*]
mon *n.* man 4, 97, 104*; **monnes** *gen.* 163, 234, 240 +; **men** *pl.* men, people 58, 125, 140 + [OE *man*]
mony *adj.* many 11, 39, 41 +; *as n.* many people 53, 63, 114 [OE *monig*]
monlokest *adj. superl.* most humane 250 [OE *mannlic*]
more *adv.* more 230, 104, 341; *n.* in *þe* ~ people of higher status 247; **moste** *adv. superl.* most of all 269 [OE *māra*]
morowen *n.* morning 307 [OE *morgen*]
morte *n.* death 247* [OF *mort*]
motes *n. pl.* spots 86 [OE *mot*]
moulyng *n.* mould 86 [cf. ON *mygla*]
mountes *pr. 3 sg.* amounts 160 [OF *monter*]
mournyng *n.* mourning, sorrow 350 [OE *murnung*]
mouth *v.* speak, pronounce 54 [from OE *mūþ*]
murthe *n.* joy 335, **myrthe** 350 [OE *myrgþ*]
muset *pa. pl.* hesitated, were in doubt 54 [OF *muser*]

nay *adv.* no 265 [ON *nei*]
naytyd *pp.* recited 119* [ON *neyta*]
nakyd *adj.* bare 89 [OE *nacod*]
name *see* **nome**
nas *pa. 3 sg.* was not 285 [OE *nam* etc. from *ne eam*]
ne *conj.* nor 102, 149, 152 + [OE *ne*]
neuenyd *pp.* named 25, spoken of 195 [ON *nefna*]
neuer *adv.* never 156, 166, 199 +, ~ *so* however 72, 239 [OE *nǣfre*]
new *adj.* new 38 [OE *nēow*]
newe *adv.* anew 6*, 14, 37* [OE *nēowe*]
ny3t *n.* night 117, 119 [OE *niht*]
no *adj.* no 148, 150, 170 +; *adv. with comp.* 169, 179, 341 + [OE *nā*]
noble *adj.* noble, grand 38, 227 [OF *noble*]
no3t *n.* nothing 56, in vain 101, ~ *bot* only 208 [OE *nōwiht*]
no3t *adv.* not 1, not at all 261 [as prec.]
noy *n.* suffering 289 [from OF *anoi*]

noyce *n.* noise 62, 218 [OF *noise*]
nombre *n.* number 206, **nommbre** group of people 289 [OF *nombre*]
nome *n.* name 16, 152, 318, **name** 18, 195; **nomes** *pl.* 18 [OE *nama, noma*]
non *adv.* not at all 157 [OE *nān*]
non(e) *pron.* no-one 101, 241, not one 289 [OE *nān*]
nones *n.* in *for þe* ~ for the purpose 38 219 [early ME *for þan anes*]
not *adv.* not 74, 97, 185 [from *nouȝt*]
note *n.* structure 38, business, fuss 101, occupation 152 [OE *notu*]
notes *n. pl.* musical notes 133 [OF *note*]
noþir, nothyre *adv.* neither 102, either 152, 199 [OE *nāhwæþer*]
notyd *pp.* recorded 103 [OF *noter*]
nourne *v.* declare, say 101, ~ *of* mention 152; **nournet** *pp.* addressed 195 [cf. Swedish *norna*, 'speak secretly']
now *adv.* now 19, 25, 33 + [OE *nū*]

of *prep.* of 19, 28, 30 + made of 48, away from 167, with respect to 172, from 127, 192 (2), 336, about 273, some of 295 [OE *of*]
ofte *adv.* often 135, 232 [OE *oft*]
olofte *adv.* on top 49 [ON *á lofti*]
on *prep.* on 2, 46, 68 +, among 73, in 77, 105 [OE *on*]
on(e) *adj.* one, a single 6, 156, 319; *pron.* 323, ~ *þe vnhapnest* the most unfortunate 198 [OE *ān*]
ones *n.* in *at* ~ simultaneously 352 [OE *ǣnes*]
one-vnder *adv.* underneath 70 [OE *on + under*]
openly *adv.* visibly 90 [from next]
opon *adj.* open 128 [OE *open*]
opon *adv.* upon 125; *prep.* upon 76, 171, into 92, **vpon** upon 202, 290, 317 [OE *up + on*]
or *conj.* or 121, **oþir** 20, 22, ~ ... ~ either ... or 86 [OE *ōþer*]
othir *adj.* other 346; **othire** *pron.* others, 32, 59, **oþir** another person 93 [as prec.]
ouerdrofe *pa. 3 sg.* passed away 117 [OE *oferdrīfan*]
oure, oureselfe *see* we
out(e) *adv.* out 9, 167, 292 +, ~ *of* 158, 292, **owt(e)** 17 [OE *ūt*]

payne *n.* suffering 333 [OF *peine*]
payntyd *pp.* painted 75 [OF *peindre*, pp. *peint*]
paynym *n.* pagan 285; **paynymes** *gen. pl.* pagans' 203 [OF *painime*]
palais *n.* palace 115 [OF *palais*]
paradis *n.* heaven 161 [OF *paradis*]
parage *n.* noble lineage 203 [OF *parage*]
partyd *pp.* gone away 107 [OF *partir*]
passyd *pa. 3 sg.* passed, went 115, 138, 141; *pl.* 351; *pp.* surpassed 163 [OF *passer*]

pepul(l) *n.* people 10, 217, 296, 351, populace 109 [OF *pueple*]
perle *n.* pearl 79 [OF *perle*]
peruertyd *pa. pl.* corrupted 10 [OF *pervertir*]
pes *n.* peace, silence 115 [AN *pes*]
picchit *pa. 3 sg.* placed 79 [uncertain]
pinchid *pa. pl.* pressed, squeezed 70 [OF *pincer*]
pyne *n.* difficulty, discomfort 141, suffering 188 [Lat *poena*, OE *pīn*]
place *n.* place, country 10, 228, building (i.e. St Paul's) 144, 153 [OF *place*]
planed *pp.* polished 50 [OF *planer*]
plantyd *pa. 3 sg.* established 13 [OE *plantian*, from Lat *plantare*]
playn *n.* floor, pavement 138 [OF *plain*]
plied *pa. pl.* bowed 138 [OF *plier*]
ply3tles *adj.* blameless 296 [from next]
plite *n.* covenant 285 [OE *pliht*]
poysned *pp.* poisoned 296 [OF *poisonner*]
pontificals *n. pl.* bishop's vestments 130 [Lat *pontificalis*]
pope *n.* pope 12 [OE, from Lat *papa*]
porer *comp. adj. as n.* poorer person 153 [AN *poure*]
powdere *n.* powder, dust 344 [OF *poudre*]
power *n.* control, jurisdiction 228 [AN *poer*]
praysid *pp.* praised, honoured 29 [OE *preisier*]
prece *n.* crowd 141 [OF *presse*]
prechyd *pa. 3 sg.* preached 13 [OF *prechier*]
precious *adv.* precious 79 [OF *precios*]
prelacie *n.* prelates, group of clergy 107 [AN *prelacie*]
prelate *n.* bishop 130, 138 [OF *prelat*]
prestly *adv.* promptly 120 [from OF *prest*]
primate *n.* bishop 107 [OF *primat*]
prince *n.* prince 203, i.e. God 161 [OF *prince*]
prises *n. pl.* levers 70 [OF *prise*]
procession *n.* procession 351 [OF *procession*]
prouidens *n.* divine power 161 [OF *providence*]
psalmyde *pp.* written as psalms 277 [from OE *psalm*, Lat *psalmus*]
pure *adj.* pure, unalloyed 13 [OF *pur*]
putten *pa. pl.* put, placed 70, **putte** *pp.* 153, 228 [uncertain]

quat *pron.* what 54, 68, 301; *adj.* what 94, 186, 187 [OE *hwæt*]
quaynt *adj.* elegant 133 [OF *queinte*]
queme *adj.* delightful 133 [OE *(ge)cwēme*]
quen *conj.* when 57, 65, 128 + [OE *hwænne*]
quere *n.* choir 133 [OF *quer*]
quere *adv.* where 274, 279 [OE *hwǣr*]
questis *n. pl.* musical sounds 133 [OF *queste*]

queþer *adv.* although, yet 153; *conj.* whether 188 [OE *hwæþere*]
quy *adv.* why 186, 222, 223 [OE *hwī*]
quil *conj.* while, as long as 215, 217 [OE *hwīl*]
quile *n.* while, short time 105 [as prec.]
quo *pron.* who 197, qwo 185 [OE *hwā*]
quod *pa. 3 sg.* said 146, 159, 225 + [OE *cweþan*]
quontyse *n.* marvel 74 [OF *cointise*]

radly *adv.* quickly 62 [OE *hrædlīce*]
raght, raȝt *pa. 3 sg.* granted 280, 338; *pl.* 256 [OE *rǣcan*]
rayked *pa. 3 sg.* went, proceeded 139 [ON *reika*]
rattes *n. pl.* tatters 260 [cf. ON *hrati*]
reame *n.* realm 11, 135 [OF *reaume*]
rede *adj.* red 91 [OE *rēad*]
redeles *adj.* directionless, in confusion 164 [OE *rǣdlēas*]
redes *pr. 3 sg.* governs, directs 192 [OE *rǣdan*]
redy *adj.* capable, wise 245 [from OE *rǣde*]
refetyd *pp.* refreshed 304 [AN *refeter*]
regne *n.* reign 212 [OF *reigne*]
regnyd *pa. 3 sg.* reigned 151 [OF *reigner*]
reken *adj.* upright, honest 245; rekenest *superl.* noblest 135 [OE *recen*]
relefe *n.* release, deliverance 328 [OF *relief*]
remewit *pa. 1 sg.* departed 235 [OF *remuer*]
renaide *pp.* apostate, renegade 11 [OF *renaier*]
renke *n.* man, person 239, 275; renkes *pl.* humans 271 [OE *rinc*, ON *rekkr*]
rent *pp.* torn 260 [OE *rendan*]
repairen *pr. pl.* visit, go 135 [OF *repairer*]
reson *n.* justice 267, by ~ according to judgement 235; reson(e)s *pl.* words 52, reasoning powers 164 [OF *resoun*]
restorment *n.* restoration 280 [OF *restorement*]
reule *v.* rule, control 231; rewlit *pa. 3 sg.* ruled 212 [OF *reuler*]
reuele *v.* reveal a mystery 121 [OF *reveler*]
reuerence *n.* deference 338; reuerens *gen.* in for ~ sake out of deference, veneration 239 [OF *reverence*]
reuestid *pp.* vested 139 139 [OF *revestir*]
rewardes *pr. 3 sg.* rewards 275; rewardid *pa. 1 sg.* rewarded 256 [AN *rewarder*]
rialle *adj.* opulent 77* [AN *rial*]
riche *adj.* rich, costly 77, 83, 280, powerful 212, 239, 267; *adv.* richly 139 [OE *rīce*, OF *riche*]
richely *adv.* sumptuously 304 [as prec.]
riȝt(e) *n.* rectitude, what is right 232*, 235, 241*, 256 +, justice 271; riȝtes *pl.* just actions 269 [OE *riht*]
riȝt(e) *adv.* justly 275, 301*, ~ now just now 332 [OE *rihte*]

ry3twis *adj.* just 245 [OE *rihtwīs*]
ryne *v.* touch 262 [OE *hrīnan*]
ryngande *adj.* resounding 62* [OE *hringan*]
rises *pr. 3 sg.* rises 344 [OE *rīsan*]
rode *n.*¹ complexion 91 [OE *rudu*]
rode *n.*² cross 290 [OE *rōd*]
roynyshe *adj.* mysterious, rune-like 52 [? from OE *rūn*]
ronge *pa. 3 sg.* rang 117 [OE *hringan*]
ronke *adj.* rebellious 11, fresh 91, foul 262 [OE *ranc*]
ronnen *pa. pl.* ran 62 [ON *renna*]
rose *n.* rose 91 [OE *rōse*]
rote *n.* rot 262 [from OE *rotian*]
roten *adj.* rotten 344 [cf. ON *rotinn*]
rotid *pp.* rotted 260 [OE *rotian*]
rottok *n.* decayed matter 344 [? from prec.]
route *n.* group 62 [OF *route*]
routhe *n.* pity 240 [from OE *hrēow*]
row *n.* in *on* ~ in a row 52 [uncertain]
rowme *n.* place at table 338 [OE *rūm*]

sacryd *pp. adj.* consecrated, holy 3, 159 [OF *sacrer*]
sacrifices *n. pl.* sacrificial rites 30 [OF *sacrifice*]
sadde *adj.* solemn, reverent 324 [OE *sæd*]
say *v.* say 100, 197; say(e)s *pr. 2 sg.* 159, 273; 3 sg. 277; *imp. sg.* say tell 279; sayd(e) *pa. 3 sg.* said 122, 273*, 282 +; *pp.* said 189, recited 136, ~ causes actions brought to trial 202 [OE *secgan*]
saynt *n.* saint 4, 12, 19 +; sayntes *pl.* 17 [OF *saint*]
sayntuaré *n.* sanctuary 66 [OF *saintuarie*]
sake *n.* sake 239 [ON *sǫk*, OE *sacu*]
same *adj.* same 204 [ON *samr*]
saule *see* soule
sauyoure *n.* saviour, i.e. Christ 324 [OF *sauveour*]
sawe *n.* speech, words 184 [OE *sagu*]
schedde *see* sheddes
schewyd *see* shewid
se *v.* see 293; *pr. pl.* 170; 3. *sg. subj.* 308; sene *pp.* seen 100 [OE *sēon*]
seche *v.* seek 41, 170 [OE *sēcan*]
sege *n.* seat, episcopal throne 35 [OF *sege*]
segge *n.* person, man 100, 159, 189 + [OE *secg*]
sele *n.* happiness 279 [OE *sǣl*]
semely *adj.* lovely 84; *adv.* fittingly 35 [ON *sœmiligr*]
semes *pr. 3 sg.* seems 98 [ON *sóma*]
send(e) *v.* send 172; *pa. 3 sg.* sent order 111; *pp.* sent 8, 12 [OE *sendan*]

septre, septure *n.* sceptre 84, 222, 256 [OF *sceptre*]
seruice *n.* religious service 136 [OF *service*]
seruyd *pp.* deserved 275 [from OF *deservir*]
sesyd *pp.* in possession, established 345 [OF *seisir*]
sett(e) *pp.* dedicated 21, placed 84, 332, ~ *of* dedicated to 24 [OE *settan*]
seuen *num.* seven 155 [OE *seofon*]
sewid *pa. 3 sg.* followed 204 [AN *suer*]
sextene *n.* sexton, sacristan 66 [OF *secrestein*]
shal *pr. 1 sg.* shall 174; **shall** *3 sg.* 347; **shulde** *pa. 3 sg.* might 54*, would be 255; **shuld** *pl.* should 42 [OE *sceal, scolde*]
sheddes *pr. or pa. 2 sg.* shed 329; **schedde** *pa. 3 sg.* 182 [OE *scēadan*]
shewid *pa. pl.* showed, were revealed 90; **schewyd** *pp.* shown 180 [OE *scēawian*]
shope *pa. 3 sg.* prepared 129; **shapen** *pp.* fashioned 88 [from OE *scieppan*]
shulde *see* **shal(l)**
sike *v.* sigh 305; **syked** *pa. 3 sg.* sighed 323; *pp.* 189 [OE *sīcan*]
synagoge *n.* heathen temple 21 [OF *sinagoge*]
synge *v.* sing 129; **songen** *pp.* 128 [OE *singan*]
sir *n.* sir (title of a priest) 108, 118, 225 [OF *sire*]
sythen *adv.* ago 1, 260; *conj.* after 2, since, because 180, 185, 222 [OE *siþþan*]
sytte *v.* sit, remain 305, sit in judgement 202; **syttes** *pr. 3 sg.* sits 35, 293 [OE *sittan*]
skelton *pr. pl.* hasten 278 [? ON]
skilfulle *adj.* righteous, just 278 [from ON *skil*]
slekkyd *pa. 3 sg.* relieved, put an end to 331 [ON *sløkkva*]
slent *n.* splash 331 [cf. ON *sletta* v.]
slepe *n.* sleep 92 [OE *slǣpan*]
slippid *pp.* slipped 92 [prob. Middle Low German *slippen*]
slode *pa. 3 sg.* fell 331 [OE *slīdan*]
so *adv.* so, therefore 23, 169, *as intensive* 45, 126, so greatly 75, so much 95, 158, in that way 258, such 150, as a result 303 [OE *swā*]
sodanly, sodenly *adv.* suddenly 92, 342 [from AN *sodein*]
solemply *adv.* reverently 129, ceremoniously 336 [from next]
solempne *adj.* sacred 303; **solempnest** *superl.* 30 [OF *solempne*]
sone *adv.* at once 58, 72, *as* ~ *as* as soon as 345 [OE *sōna*]
songen *see* **synge**
soper *n.* supper 303, 308, 332 [OF *soper*]
sorow(e) *n.* sorrow 305, 309, 327 [OE *sorh*]
soth(e) *n.* truth 159, 170, 197 [OE *sōþ*]
sothe *adj.* true 277 [OE *sōþ*]
soule *n.* soul 279, 293, 300 +, **saule** 273 [OE *sāwol*]
soun *n.* voice 324, **sowne** 341 [AN *soun*]
sounde *n.* good health 92 [OE *gesund* adj.]

soupen *pr. pl.* dine 336 [OF *souper*]
souerayn *n.* sovereign Lord 120 [OF *soverain*]
space *n.* time 93, 312 [OF *(e)space*]
spakly *adv.* quickly 335, copiously 312 [ON *spakliga*]
speche *n.* word 152 [OE *spēc*]
spede *n.* success 132 [OE *spēd*]
spedeles *adj.* useless 93 [OE *spēd* + *lēas*]
speke *v.* speak 312; **spake** *pa. 3 sg.* 217 [OE *specan*]
spelunke *n.* coffin, tomb 49, 217 [Lat *spelunca*]
sperl *n.* lid 49 [cf. Middle Dutch *sperrelen*]
spyr *v.* ask 93 [OE *spyrian*]
spyrit *n.* spirit 335 [AN *spirit*]
spradde *pa. 3 sg.* closed 49 [OE *gesparrian*]
sprange *pa. 3 sg.* arose 217 [OE *springan*]
sprent *pa. 3 sg.* leapt 335 [cf. ON *spretta*]
stablyd *pa. 3 sg.* established 2, *pp.* settled 274 [OF *(e)stablir*]
stadde *pp.* placed 274 [ON *staddr*]
stille *adj.* still, quiet 219 [OE *stille*]
ston *n.* stone 47, 219; **stones** *pl.* 40 [OE *stān*]
stondes *pr. 3 sg.* stands 164; **stode** *pa. 3 sg.* remained 97; **stode(n)** *pl.* stood 52, 219, were present 73 [OE *stondan*]
stoundes *n. pl.* times 288 [OE *stund*]
strange *adj.* strange, remarkable 74 [OF *stra(u)nge*]
stre3t *adv.* correctly 274 [OE *streht*, pp. of *streccan*]
such(e) *adj.* such 97, 110, 146 +, these 178 [OE *swilc*]
suffrid pa. 3 sg. suffered 2 [AN *suffrir*]
sum(me) *adj.* some 100, 192, 276 [OE *sum*]
sutile *adj.* graceful 132 [OF *sutil*]
swarues *pr. 3 sg.* swerves 167 [OE *sweorfan*]
swete *adj.* sweet 120, 342 [OE *swēte*]
swyndid *pa. 3 sg.* faded away 342 [OE *swindan*]

table *n.* table 332 [OF *table*]
take *v.* take on, undertake 168, **take** *pr. pl.* in ~ in ingest 297; **toke** *pa. 3 sg.* in ~ hym seized 313; **token** *pl.* in ~ to reached 57 [ON *taka*]
tale *n.* verbal report, story 102, 109 [OE *talu*]
talent *n.* wish, desire 176 [OF *talent*]
talkes *pr. 3 sg.* talks 177 [? from OE *talu*]
tecche *n.* stain 85 [OF *teche*]
teches *pr. 3 sg.* teaches 34 [OE *tǣcan*]
telle *v.* relate 114* [OE *tellan*]
temple *n.* (heathen) temple 5, 28, 31 +; **temples** *pl.* 15 [OE *templ* from Lat, OF *temple*]

temyd *pa. 3 sg.* owed allegiance to 15 [OE *tēman*]
tene *n.* suffering 331 [OE *tēona*]
teres *n. pl.* tears 314, 322 [OE *tēar*]
tethe *n. pl.* teeth 297 [OE *tōþ*, pl. *tēþ*]
þagh *conj.* although 122, 243, 244 + [OE *þēah*]
þai *pron.* they 9, 43, 248 + (*and see* hom, hor) [ON *þeir*]
thar *pr. 3 sg.* may 262 [OE *þearf*]
þat *dem. pron.* that 4, 5, 6 +, by ~ by the time that, when 113; *rel. pron.* that, which, who 8, 10, 24 +, what 25, that which 166 [OE *þæt*]
þat *conj.* that 100, 226, (expressing result) 64, so that 42, 175, 310 + [as prec.]
þe *def. art.* the 5, 8, 9 +, The 49*, 111 [OE *þe*]
the *see* þou
þen *adv.* then, (at) that time 11, 13, 73 +, þenne 118*, 212* [OE *þenne*]
þen *conj.* than 230, 270 [OE *þænne*]
thenke *pr. 1 sg.* intend 225 [OE *þencan*]
ther *adv.* there 3, 39, 52 +, þere 94*, 292*; *conj.* where 138, 304 [OE *þǣr, þāra*]
þerafter *adv.* afterwards 189 [OE *þǣr æfter*]
þereas *conj.* where 167 [OE *þǣr + ealswa*]
þerinne *adv.* in there 27 [OE *þǣrinne*]
þerof *adv.* for that 339 [OE *þǣrof*]
þeronne *adv.* upon it 79* [OE *þǣron*]
þeroute *adv.* out of there 291 211 [OE *þǣrūte*]
þertille *adv.* to that place 69* [OE *þǣr* + ON *til*]
þerto *adv.* to that place 59, 70 [OE *þǣrtō*]
þi *see* þou
þider *adv.* to there 58, 63, 135 [OE *þider*]
þiderwarde(s) *adv.* to that place 61, 112 [OE *þiderweardes*]
thykke *adj.* thick, solid 47 [OE *þicce*]
thynkes *impers.* in me ~ it seems to me 259 [OE *þyncan*]
þis *pron. & adj.* this 11, 98, 125 +; þes *adj.* these 155, 317 [OE *þes* etc.]
þof *conj.* though, even if 320 (cf. þagh) [ON *þó*]
þou *pron.* you 159, 179, 181 +, þow 186; the 276, 326; þi your 124, 193, 194 +, þin 330; þiselwen yourself 185 [OE *þū* etc.]
þousand *adj.* thousand 210 [OE *þūsend*]
threnen *adj.* three times 210 [? cf. ON *þrennr*]
thrid *adj.* third 31 [OE *þridda*]
þritty *adj.* thirty 210 [OE *þrītig*]
thryuandly *adv.* skilfully 47 [from ON *þrífask*]
throgh *n.* coffin 47 [OE *þrūh*]
thurgh *prep.* through, by means of 123, 192 [OE *þurh*]
þus *adv.* thus 99, 186, 189 +, in this way 271 [OE *þus*]
til(l) *conj.* until 12, 136, 313 [ON *til*]

tyme *n.* time 5, 15, 24 + [OE *tīma*]
tithynges *n. pl.* tidings, news 57 [OE *tīdung*, ON *tíðendi*]
title *n.* legal rights 28, inscription 102 [OF *title*]
to *adv.* too 206(1) [OE *tō*]
to *prep.* to 23, 57, 105 +, (introducing infin.) in order to 6, 108 [as prec.]
today *adv.* today 180 [OE *tō dæg*]
token *n.* visible sign 102 [OE *tācn*]
toke(n) *see* **take**
tolden *pa. pl.* related 109; **tolde** *pp.* reckoned 31, related 36 [OE *tellan*]
toles *n. pl.* tools 40 [OE *tōl*]
tome *n.* opportunity 313 [ON *tóm*]
torent *pp.* torn apart 164 [OE *torendan*]
toumbe *n.* tomb 46, 139, 177 +; ~ -*wonder* miraculous tomb 57 [OF *tombe*]
toun *n.* town 5, 34, 57 + [OE *tūn*]
toward *prep.* relative to, compared with 161 [OE *tōweard*]
trewe *adj. as n.* faithful ones 336* [OE *trēowe*]
trillyd *pa. pl.* streamed 322 [? ON]
tronyd *pp.* enthroned 255 [from OF *trone* n.]
troubull *n.* agitation, disturbance 109 [OF *truble*]
trouthe *n.* true faith 13, true fact 184, what is just 268 [OE *trēowþ*]
trowid *pa. 3 sg.* believed 204; *pp.* 255 [OE *trēowian*]
tulkes *n. pl.* people 109 [ON *túlkr*]
turnes *pr. 3 sg.* turns 177; **turnyd** *pa. 3 sg.* converted 15 [OE *turnian*]
twayne *n.* two 32 [OE *twēgen*]
two *adj.* two 91 [OE *twā*]

vche *adj.* each 204, ~ *a* every 275, 348, **vschon** *pron.* each person 93 [OE *ǣlc*, *ǣlc + ān*]
vghten *n.* dawn 118 [OE *ūhtan*]
vnchaungit *pp.* unaltered 95 [OE *un-* + OF *changer*]
vnclosid *pa. pl.* opened 140 [OE *un-* + OF *clos* n.]
vnder *prep.* under 166, subject to 203, 227 [OE *under*]
vnhapnest *adj. superl.* most unfortunate 198 [from ON *heppinn*]
vnknawen *pp.* unknown 147 [OE *un-* + *gecnāwen*]
vnlouke *v.* unfasten 67, release 162 [OE *unlūcan*]
vnpreste *adj.* unprepared 285 [from OF *prest*]
vnsaȝt *adj.* hostile, warlike 8 [from OE *sæht*]
vnskathely *adj.* innocent 278 [cf. ON *skaði*]
vnsparid *adj.* unrestrained 335 [OE *un-* + *sparian*]
vnwemmyd *pp. adj.* unstained 96, 266 [OE *unwemmed*]
vnworthi *adj.* unworthy 122 [from OE *worþ* n.]
vp *adv.* up 178, out of bed 118 [OE *up*]

vphalden *pp.* upraised 349 [OE *up + haldan*]
vpon *see* opon; vs *see* we; vschon *see* vche
vsen *pr. pl.* practice 270; vsit *pa. 2 sg.* 187; *3 sg.* inhabited 200 [OF *user*]

vayles *pr. 3 sg.* avails, is worth 348 [OF *valoir*]
vayneglorie *n.* vanity 348 [OF *vaine gloire*]
verray *adj.* precise 53 [AN *verrai*]
verrayly *adv.* truthfully 174 [from prec.]
vertue *n.* power 286; vertues *pl.* 174 [OF *vertu*]
vigures *n. pl.* figures, characters 53 [OF *figure*]
visite *v.* carry out a visitation 108 [OF *visiter*]
visoun *n.* vision 121 [OF *vision*]
vouchesafe *v.* vouchsafe, condescend to grant 121 [OF *voucher + sauf*]

waggyd *pa. 3 sg.* shook 281 [OE *wagian*]
wakenyd *pa. 3 sg.* sprang up 218 [OE *wacian*]
wale *n. or v.* in *to ~* in abundance, very much 73 [ON *val*]
walon *pp.* arrived, gathered 64 [from prec.]
wan *pa. pl.* gained 301 [OE *gewinnan*]
warpyd *see* werpe; was *see* be
water *n.* water 316, 329, 333 [OE *wæter*]
we *pron.* we 155, 156, 169 +; vs us 185, 212, 294 +; oure our 21, 154, 155 +;
    oureselfe ourselves 170 [OE *wē, ūs, ūre*]
wede *n.* clothing 96; wedes *pl.* clothes 77, 85 [OE *wǣd*]
weghe *n.* person 96, 186; wehes *pl.* people 73 [OE *wiga*]
weldes *pr. 3 sg.* rules 161[OE *wealdan*]
wele *n.* wealth, riches 233 [OE *wela*]
wele *adv.* well, fully 183 [OE *wel*]
wele-dede *n.* good deeds 301 [OE *weldǣd*]
welnegh *adv.* nearly 119 [OE *wel-nēh*]
wemles *adj.* spotless, unsullied 85 [OE *wamm + -lēas*]
wenten *pa. pl.* went 69 [OE *wendan*]
wepand *pr. p.* weeping 122; wepid *pa. pl.* 220, 310 [OE *wēpan*]
were *see* be
weres *pr. 2 sg.* wear 222 [OE *werian*]
werke *n.* work 61 [OE *we(o)rc*]
werkemen *n. pl.* workmen, labourers 69 [from prec.]
werpe *pa. 2 sg.* uttered 329, warpyd *pa. 3 sg.* 321 [OE *weorpan*]
werre *n.* war 215 [AN *werre*]
wesche *pa. pl.* washed 333 [OE *wæscan*]
wete *n.* water 321 [OE *wǣt*]
wy3t *adj.* strong 69 [ON *vígt*]
wille *n.* wish 226 [OE *willa*]

wynter *n. pl.* years 230 [OE *winter*]
wyrke *v.* work 39; **wroghtes** *pa. 2 sg.* behaved 274; **wroghtyn** *pl.* acted 301; **wroght** *pp.* carried out 226 [OE *wyrcan*]
wise *n.* manner 77, 229, *in no* ~ no way 263 [OE *wīse*]
witere *imp.* inform 185 [ON *vitra*]
wyterly *adv.* for certain 183 [from ON *vitr*]
with *prep.* with 40, 48, 65 +, ~ *þat* then 69, **wyt** 165, 341 [OE *wiþ*]
within(ne) *prep.* within 64; *adv.* inside 68, 75, *me* ~ in my heart 252 [OE *wiþinnan*]
withouten *prep.* without 85 [OE *wiþūtan*]
wold *pa. pl.* wished to 68 [OE *willan, wolde*]
wonder *n.* amazement 73, 220, marvel 57, 99, 106 [OE *wundor*]
wondres *pr. pl.* wonder 125 [OE *wundrian*]
wonnes *pr. 3 sg.* dwells, resides 279 [OE *wunian*]
wontyd *pa. pl.* were lacking 208 [ON *vanta*]
woo *n.* sorrow 310 [OE *wā*]
worde *n.* word 218, 321; **wordes** *pl.* words 56, 178, 191 + [OE *word*]
worlde *n.* world 64, 186, *in al þis* ~ anywhere 218 [OE *woruld*]
wormes *n. pl.* maggots 262 [OE *wyrm*]
worthe *v.* happen, come to pass 258; *pr. 2 sg. subj.* be 340*; **worthyn** *pp.* become, been 330 [OE *weorþan*]
wos *see* **be**
wost *pr. 2 sg.* know 183; **wot** *pl.* 185 [OE *witan*]
wothe *n.* danger 233 [ON *váði*]
wrakeful *adj.* vengeful 215 [from OE *wracu*]
wrang *adj.* wrong, false 236 [late OE *wrang* from ON]
wranges *n. pl.* wrongs 243 [as prec.]
wrath(e) *n.* anger 215, hostility 233 [OE *wrǣþþu*]
writtes *n. pl.* writings 277 [OE *writ*]
wroghtes *see* **wyrke**

Index of Names

Adam 295
Appolyn Apollo 19
Austyn Saint Augustine 12;
　Augustynes *gen.* 33

Belyn Belinus 213
Berynge Brennius, brother of
　Belinus 213
Bretaynes *gen.* Britain's 31
Breton Briton 213; *pl.* Bretons 9
Brutus Brutus 207

Crist(e) Jesus Christ 2, 209; **Cristes**
　gen. 16

Englond 1
Erkenwolde 4, 33, 108 +
Esex Essex 108

Hengystes *gen.* Hengist's 7*

James St James the apostle 22
Jesu(s) Jesus Christ 22, 180

Jono Juno (wife of Jupiter) 22
Jubiter Jupiter 22

London 1, 25, 34

Mahoun Mahomet 20
Margrete St Margaret 20
Maudelayne St Mary Magdalen 20

Paule, Saynte St Paul's Cathedral 113
Petre St Peter 19

Sandewich 12
Sathanas *gen.* Satan's 24
Saxones 8; *as adj.* 30*
Sonne Sun god 21

Triapolitan *adj.* 36; *as n.*
　Triapolitanes 31
Troye i.e. ancient London 246, 251,
　255; **New Troie** 25, 211

Wales 9

www.ingramcontent.com/pod-product-compliance
Lightning Source LLC
Chambersburg PA
CBHW071412300426
44114CB00016B/2276